The Three Distinct Knocks
along with
Jachin and Boaz

by Samuel Pritchard

Foreword by
Michael R. Poll

A Cornerstone Book

The Three Distinct Knocks
along with
Jachin and Boaz
by Samuel Pritchard
Foreword by
Michael R. Poll

A Cornerstone Book
Published by Cornerstone Book Publishers
Copyright © 2020-2024 by Michael R. Poll

Cornerstone Book Publishers
Hot Springs Village, AR
www.cornerstonepublishers.com
1cornerstonebooks@gmail.com

First Cornerstone Edition – 2020

ISBN: 9781613423479

Foreword

Speculative Freemasonry was born out of the desire to preserve the philosophical and moral teachings of the old Operative Freemasons. The old "workers in stone" were not only builders of cathedrals, but also builders of humanity. They took good, decent candidates and with the education necessary to give them the skills of Master Builders, they also provided them with the path to becoming better human beings. It was this additional training that was felt to be of such great value to the whole of humanity when the building trades began to decline, and the lodges of Operatives began to fade away. The loss of this philosophical education was felt to be unacceptable.

The Renaissance led into the Age of Enlightenment. It was times of great change and self-discovery. Men with no desire at all to enter the building trade, found great value in the moral lessons of the old Operatives. Slowly, these non-Operatives began to find their way into the lodges which once only admitted actual builders or builders in training. While these new members possessed no interest in learning building, they found great wisdom in the lessons of life. They were also intrigued by the ritualistic way these lessons were delivered. With the flavor of alchemy and every science known to man, these ethical plays were provided in a manner to offer the members a chance at spiritual and moral growth. This amazing approach to imparting enlightenment could not be allowed to die along with the building guilds. *Speculative Freemasons* began to save the heart and metaphysical soul of the old Operatives.

Because of the true hunger society possessed for inner growth, the Masonic manner of teaching struck a chord within all who became aware of Speculative Freemasonry's existence. Lodges of Speculative Freemasons soon popped up all over

Europe and then all over the world. The ritual used to deliver the lessons soon evolved to reflect the nature of the societies using the rituals.

In 1723, a London newspaper published what would seem to be the very first Masonic exposure. In 1760, Samuel Pritchard expanded the untitled work to include the opening and closing of the lodge and released the exposure as *The Three Distinct Knocks*. Offered in this book is a digitally enhanced photographic reproduction of the 1760 edition of Pritchard's work. This is a significant work for all Masons, as it provides us with a clear look at the early roots of our Masonic ritual. Along with this publication, is Pritchard's 1797 companion piece, *Jachin and Boaz*.

Masonic ritual is the vehicle used by Freemasonry to deliver the symbolic lessons presented to the candidates. Over time, these rituals, or lessons, are changed, tweaked, modified and molded to match the times and societies where they are used. While the core of the lessons remains the same, the packaging is often varied. Cornerstone is proud to present this important work for your examination and study.

Michael R. Poll
Cornerstone Book Publishers

The Three Distinct Knocks

THE
Three diſtinct Knocks,
Or the Door of the moſt
ANTIENT FREE-MASONRY,
Opening to all Men,
Neither Naked nor Cloath'd,
Bare-foot nor ſhod, &c.

Being an Univerſal Deſcription of all its Branches,

FROM

Its firſt Riſe to this preſent Time,

As it is deliver'd in all Lodges :

CONTAINING,

I. The Author's Reaſons for opening the Door of Maſonry to all the World.

II. How to open a Lodge and ſet the Men to Work.

III. Giving an exact Account of all their Proceedings in the making a Brother, with the Three Obligations or Oaths belonging to the Firſt, Second, and Third Degrees of Maſonry, viz. The Enter'd Apprentice, and Fellow-Craft, and Maſter-Maſon; with the Obligation belonging to the Chair, and the Gripe and Word.

IV. The Form of a Lodge; with a full Deſcription of the drawing upon the Floor of a Lodge, with the Three Steps, and a Prayer uſed at the making of a Brother; with Songs to be ſung after grave Buſineſs is done.

V. The Examination of a Brother, whereby he may get Admittance into a Lodge, without going through the Obligations : With all the Words explained that belongs to the Gripe.

VI. A new and accurate Liſt of all the ENGLISH regular Lodges in the World, according to their Seniority, with the Dates of each Conſtitution and Days of Meeting.

By *W—— O—— V——n* :
Member of a Lodge in *England* at this Time.

The SEVENTH EDITION.

LONDON:
Printed for H. SERJEANT, without *Temple-Bar*.

1

✳✳✳✳✳✳✳✳✳✳✳✳✳✳✳✳✳✳✳✳✳✳✳✳

THE

EXPLANATION

OF THE

FOLLOWING FIGURE,

which is all the

Drawing that is ufed in this Sort of Mafonry,

CALLED,

The Moſt ANTIENT by the *Iriſhmen*.

IT is generally done with Chalk, or Charcoal, on the Floor ; that is the Reafon that they want a Mop and Pail fo often
as they do : before when a Man has been made
a Mafon, they wafh it out : but People have
taken Notice, and made Game of them about
the Mop and Pail : So fome Lodges ufe Tape
and little Nails to form the fame Thing, and

a   fo

fo keep the World more ignorant of the Matter.

Note. This Plan is drawn on the Floor, Eaft and Weft: The Mafter ftands in the Eaft, with the Square about his Neck, and the Bible before him, which he takes up and walks forward to the Weft, near the firft Step of an oblong Square; where he kneels down, in order to give that folemn Obligation to him that has already knelt down, with his Left-knee bare, bent upon the firft Step; his Right-foot forms a Square, with his naked Right-hand upon the holy Bible, *&c.*

And fo to the Second and Third Degree of Mafonry; as is fhewn upon the Steps.

THE

N O T E.

ALL this Figure is waſhed out with a Mop, as aforeſaid, as ſoon as he has received the Obligation.

Then a Table is put in the Place where this Figure was, and they all ſit round it; but every Man ſitteth in the ſame Place as he ſtood before the Figure was waſhed out, *viz.* the Maſter in the Eaſt, the Senior Warden in the Weſt, *&c.*

Every Man has a Glaſs ſet him, and a large Bowl of Punch, or what they like, is ſet in in the Center of the Table; and the Senior Deacon charges (as they call it) in the North and Eaſt, and the Junior Deacon in the South and Weſt; for it is their Duty ſo to do, *i. e.* to fill all the Glaſſes.

Then the Maſter takes up his Glaſs, and gives a Toaſt to the King and the Craft, with Three Times Three in the Prentice's; and they

they all fay Ditto, and drink all together, minding the Mafter's Motion : They do the fame with the empty Glafs, that he doth ; that is, he draws it a-crofs his Throat Three Times (which is the Penalty of the Obligation of your Throat being cut a-crofs), and then makes Three Offers to put it down : At the Third, they all fet their Glaffes down together, which they call firing : Then they hold the Left-hand Breaft-high, and clap Nine Times with the Right, their Foot going at the fame Time : When this done, they all fit down.

THE

XXXXXXXXXXXXXXXXXXXXXXXXXXXXXXX

THE

Author's REASONS for opening the Door of MASONRY to all the World.

DEDICATED TO

THE RIGHT WORSHIPFUL

COMPANY OF FAITHFUL

IRISH MASTERS

Of Number I,

And the whole FRATERNITY, which it may be of Service to ———

SIRS,

I Am obliged to dedicate my Book to Number 1, becaufe they are all Mafters, and in Partnerfhip; befides, they would be angry if I did not give them that Honour; for they that are not Mafters, can't be admitted: But it may be of Service to the younger Brothers, becaufe it will let them into the Tricks that are carried on, which you can't come at under Six or Seven Years, and the Expence of a great many Pounds; but here you may learn it all in a Month, and go and lecture as well as the beft of them. But

B   if

(2)

if you belong to any Lodge, you muſt give a
Shilling every Quarter to Number I, to feaſt
their d—mn'd Guts, and perhaps your family
wanted it at home : But this Family of *Pluto*'s
have the impudence of the D—l, to ſay if you
don't ſend a Shilling when they want it, you
ſhall be excluded all Lodges whatſoever : And
thus there goes Four or Five Shillings a Year,
you don't know for what; beſides other Expences, which is ten times as much. I could
give you a Liſt of Expences for one Year only
would make you ſtare; but it does not ſignify,
for any Man that has been a Maſon Half a Year,
and comes to read this Book, will know what I
ſay to be true, and more ſo if he reads it out;
for it will let him into things he never thought
of, but now he will ſee them as plain as poſ-
ſible.

Pray, Brother, what is the matter that Six or
Eight or Ten Brethren, that like to learn Maſonry, can't meet at a Brother's Houſe when
they pleaſe, and ſpend their Sixpence with Pleaſure, and depart in Peace, without wrangling
and cheating one another; which two often happens of late, by admitting of bad Men, and
laying Charges upon them that are not honeſt
enough to keep one Tittle thereof; which I could
ſpeak of Two or Three who were made Maſters
very lately, and in a Month's Time turned
out the moſt forſworn Villains in the World.

There-

[3]

Therefore I advife all young Brethren to meet as aforefaid ; firft at one Brother's Houfe, and then at another, that is, in the public Way : For what Occafion have you to be confin'd to any particular Lodge, when you may hold a Lodge where you pleafe, and when you pleafe ; having either Three, Five, Seven or Eleven, and as many more as you pleafe ; and thus you will be of Service to one another, without fending your Money to the grand Number I, as they call it, which they tell you is for Charity ; but if it be, I am afraid they make themfelves the Poor : Thus I advife you further, that you have nothing to do with them, for they are Wolves in Sheeps Cloathing.

It was the cuftom among the Primitive Ma-fons, and alfo among the Primitive Chriftians, to vifit one another ; for it is faid as Iron fharpens Iron, fo fhall one Man fharpen another.

But methinks I hear fome young Brethren fay, Who fhall inftruct us ? I anfwer : Buy this Book, thou wilt have Inftructions enough. But per-haps you will fay, How fhall I know that it is right? Get fome faithful *Irifhman*, for Two or Three Times, and you will foon fee that this Book is right; for they all underftand Mafonry, even the loweft Clafs of them, if they are once made ; for then it is the chief of their Bufi-nefs. In the Winter they have a little Money out of

B 2 the

(4)

the Box of Number I, to buy them a few Cloaths, fo you may have one of them any Night, only paying for what he eats and drinks, for they never pay any thing; but if they can lay hold of the Money, they will: So I charge you to take care of that, and you may do well enough with them, paying their Expences of the Night: Or you may have a faithful Inftructor from Number 1; the Secretary, or the like, with One or Two with him; but they muft be all free; becaufe they come to inftruct the young Brethren; and fometimes you muft pay a Coach-hire or Waterage, or the like, according to the Situation of the Place.

Therefore it is the beft way not to be troubl'd with them, but as little as you can help; yet I would have you try, and you will find what I fay to be true; for it is by Experience. I could fay ten times more, but I don't care to be too harfh: I only give you Hints, whereby, with a little Experience, you will find it all out; and a great deal more Villainy that is carry'd on, and three Parts of the Free-Mafons know nothing about the Matter.

For they pretended to fo much Holinefs at firft when I came to *England*, I thought they were Gods, but I foon found them D---ls. For at firft I found all their pretended Friendfhip not to be real, becaufe they had fo much of it that made me fick, and I dare fay fome of you, Brethren,

(5)

thren, have been as fick with their pretended Ho-
nefty, as ever I was.

But with all their Wit, they never could find
me out, that I never was made a Mafon, or received any of the following Obligations ; yet I
have been a Member of feveral Lodges, both
Antient and Modern, and Royal Arch ; and have
been Mafter of fome Lodges in *England*. I will
tell you how I came at it without being made ; as
follows.

I am a *German*, born near *Berlin* ; and being
acquainted with an *Englifh* Family, who had a
large Quantity of Books, and being intimate with
their Children, I learnt a little *Englifh*, and took
great delight in reading of *Englifh* Books, which
I could have when I would. About the Year
1740, (I was then upwards of 20 Years old) as I
was looking in my Neighbour's Library, I found
a Pamphlet, called, *Maffonry Diffected*, an *Englifh*
Book ; I read it with great Attention, becaufe I had
heard of Mafonry to be a very bad Thing ; fo I
took great Notice of this Book, and could fay it
all by Heart, or very near, and concluded it was
the whole Thing, but it was not, yet there was
enough to get Admittance into a Lodge. For,

About Two or Three Years after, I went to
Paris ; I had not been there long, before I work'd
with a Man that was a Mafon, and belonged to a
Lodge

(6)

Lodge in *Paris*. We fell in Difcourfe about Mafonry, (I had heard that he he was one before) I afk'd him if he was a Free Mafon; he faid, are you? I faid I am; and he afk'd me where I was made, I faid at *Berlin*. He afk'd me fome Queftions, which I anfwer'd out of the Book, and happen'd to be right; fo he fhook me by the Hand and call'd me Brother, and took me to his Lodge, which I became a Member of, and belong'd to it whilft I ftaid there, which was two or three Years; then my Bufinefs led me to *England*. When I fet out, they gave me a Certificate, and was very forry to part from me, but defir'd me to remember them to all Brothers in *England*, which I did not forget. I went to a Modern Lodge, as the *Irifh* call them, whofe grand Lodge is held at the *Devil* Tavern, but I don't care to mention the Lodge. They never difputed me when I fhew'd them my Certificate, for they were fond of hearing how Mafons proceeded in other Countries, which is juft the fame as it is here, only one Thing in the Mafter's Part, and that I fhall fpeak of in the Mafter's Part. Then I was invited to an *Irifh* Lodge, that call'd themfelves the moft antient Mafons, that holds their Grand Lodge at the *Five Bell* Tavern in the *Strand*, which is the whole Subject of this Book; for which Reafon, their impudent blundering *Irifh* (*T---m T---dman*'s Cart driving) Secretary, have thought fit to ufe fuch Scurrility, to depreciate it in his nonfenfical ftupid performance, called, *A----n R--·n*: But the other I don't meddle
with

(7)

with, becaufe there is a Book already publifhed, call'd *Mafonry Diffeƈted*, which was publifhed in the Year 1700; and I believe was all the Mafonry that was made ufe of of at that Time, but it is not half that is ufed now, tho' it is the nigheft that ever was wrote about the Matter before this.

Although there have been many Books writ a-bout Mafonry, but moft to draw the Reader's Mind from off the aforefaid Book ; for I have read them all that have been publifh'd thefe Twenty Years, and I never faw any Mafonry but in the aforefaid Book. There is one publifh'd, called, *A Mafter-Key to Free Mafonry*, but it is not the Thing, tho' it is fomething about the Matter, but fo very little, that it is not worth fpeaking of ; there is not one Thing right, only fome of the Words, but not in their proper Places. I wonder that any Man can pretend to write a Book of a Thing that he knows nothing of, but by picking a Bit here there For no Man is able to fpeak or write this Secret, without he has vifited Lodges fome Years. He fpeaks of Drawing upon the Cieling with a Pencil, that fhews he knew nothing about the Matter, to fill People's Cielings full of Marks and Scratches, which would foon be known to all the World. All Men that ever faw any Thing of Mafonry, knows that their Drawing is upon the Floor, (and that is the Reafon of the Mop and Pail) but any Man that reads my Book with Attention, will find it right, by his own Judgment only ;

(8)

only ; for I will affure you there was never fuch an
exact Account before publifh'd; which I hope will
give entire Satisfaction to all Lovers of Truth; fo I
fhall remain,

Your moft obedient

Humble Servant,

W——— O——— V———n.

N. B. *The Stile of the aforefaid and following A-*
pologies may not be fo fine as it fhould, but I
hope the Reader will excufe me, as I am not
an Englifhman; *but I affure you, my Mean-*
ing is Truth and Juftice, and I hope will be
underftood.

THE

(9)

THE

Three diſtinct Knocks,

Or the Door of the moſt

ANTIENT FREE - MASONRY,

Opening to all Men, &c.

How to open the Lodge, to ſet the Men to work.

Maſter, to the junior Deacon.

WHAT is the chief care of a Maſon?
　　Anſwer. To ſee that his Lodge is tyl'd.
Maſ. Pray do your Duty.

N. B. The junior Deacon goes and gives Three
　　Knocks at the Door; and if there is no-
　　body nigh, the Tyler without anſwereth
　　with Three Knocks: The junior Deacon
　　tells the Maſter, and ſays; Worſhipful,
　　the Lodge is tyl'd.
　　　　　　　C　　　　　　　*Maſ.*

Maſ. to jun. Dea. The junior Deacon's Place in the Lodge?

Deacon's Anſ. At the Back of the ſenior Warden, or at his Right hand if he permits him.

Maſ. Your Buſineſs?

Deacon's Anſ. To carry Meſſages from the ſenior to the junior Warden, ſo that they may be diſperſed round the Lodge.

Maſ. to the ſen. Dea. The ſenior Deacon's Place in the Lodge?

Sen. Deacon's Anſ. At the Back of the Maſter, or at his Right-hand if he permits him.

Maſ. Your Buſineſs there?

Sen. Deacon's Anſ. To carry Meſſages from the Maſter to the ſenior Warden.

Maſ. The junior Warden's Place in the Lodge?

Deacon's Anſ. In the South.

Maſ. to the jun. Warden. Your Buſineſs there?

Sen. Warden's Anſ. The better to obſerve the Sun, at high Meridian, to call the Men off from Work to Refreſhment, and to ſee that they come on in due Time, that the Maſter may have Pleaſure and Profit thereby.

Maſ. The ſenior Warden's Place in the Lodge?

Jun. Warden's Anſ. In the Weſt.

Maſ. to the ſen. Warden. Your Buſineſs there?

Sen. Warden's Anſ. As the Sun ſets in the Weſt to cloſe the Day, ſo the Senior ſtands in the Weſt to cloſe the Lodge, paying the Hirelings their Wages, and diſmiſſing them from their Labour.

Maſ. The Maſter's Place in the Lodge?

Sen. Warden's Anſ. In the Eaſt.

Maſ. His Buſineſs there?

Sen. Warden's Anſ. As the Sun riſes in the Eaſt

to

(11)

o open the Day, fo the Mafter ftands in the Eaft
o open his Lodge to fet Men to Work.

N. B. Then the Mafter takes off his Hat, which
he always has on but at this Time, and puts
it on again as foon as the Lodge is open
but all the reft keep theirs off, and he de;
clares the Lodge open as follows.

Maf. This Lodge is open, in the Name of God
and holy St. *John*, forbidding all curfing and fwear-
ing, whifpering, and all prophane Difcourfe whatfoever, under no lefs Penalty than what the Majority
fhall think proper; not lefs than One Penny a
Time, nor more than Sixpence.

N. B. Then he gives Three Knocks upon the Table with a wooden Hammer, and puts on
his Hat; then they all fit down, and begin their Lecture, as follows.

The enter'd Aprentice's Lecture.

Maf. BRother, Is there any Thing between you
and I ?

Anf. There is, Worfhipful.

Maf. What is it Brother ?

Anf. A Secret.

Maf. What is it that Secret, Brother ?

Anf. Mafonry.

Maf. Then I prefume you are a Mafon ?

Anf. I am fo taken and accepted amongft Brothers and Fellows.

Maf. Pray what Manner of Man ought a Mafon Man to be ?

Anf. A Man that is born of a Free Woman.

C 2   *Maf.*

(12)

Maf. Where was you firft prepar'd to be made a Mafon ?

Anf. In my Heart.

Maf. Where was you next prepar'd ?

Anf. In a Room adjoining to the Lodge.

Maf. How was you prepar'd Brother ?

Anf. I was neither naked nor cloathed, barefoot nor fhod, depriv'd of all Metal, hoodwink'd with a cable Tow about my Neck, where I was led to the Door of the Lodge in a halting moving Pofture, by the Hand of a Friend, whom I afterwards found to be a Brother.

Maf. How did you know it to be a Door, you being blinded ?

Anf. By finding a Stoppage, and afterwards an Enterance or Admittance.

Maf. How got you Admittance ?

Anf. By three diftinct Knocks.

Maf. What was faid to you within ?

Anf. Who comes there.

Maf. Your Anfwer Brother ?

Anf. One who begs to have and receive Part of the Benefit of this right worfhipful Lodge, dedicated to St. *John*, as many Brothers and Fellows have done before me.

Maf. How do you expect to obtain it ?

Anf. By being free born and well reported.

Maf. What was faid to you then ?

Anf. Enter.

Maf. How did you enter, and upon what ?

Anf. Upon the Point of a Sword or Spear, or fome Warlike Inftrument, prefented to my left naked Breaft.   *Maf.*

(13)

Maſ. What was ſaid to you then ?

Anſ. I was aſk'd if I felt any Thing.

Maſ. What was your Anſwer ?

Anſ. I did, bnt I could ſee nothing.

Maſ. You have told me how you was received, pray who received you ?

Anſ. The Junior Warden.

Maſ. How did he dilpoſe of you ?

Anſ. He deliver'd me to the Maſter, who order'd me to kneel down and receive the Benefit of a Prayer.

Brethren, let Pray.

O Lord God, thou great and univerſal Maſon of the World, and firſt Builder of Man, as it were a Temple ; be with us, O Lord, as thou haſt promiſed, when two or three are gathered together in thy Name, thou wilt be in the midſt of them; be with us, O Lord, and bleſs all our Undertakings, and grant that this our Friend, may become a faithful Brother. Let Grace and Peace be multiplied unto him, through the Knowledge of our Lord Jeſus Chriſt : And grant, O Lord, as he putteth forth his Hand to thy Holy Word, that he may alſo put forth his Hand to ſerve a Brother but not to hurt himſelf or his Family ; that whereby may be given to us great and precious Promiſes, that by this we may be Partakers of thy divine Nature, and having eſcaped the Corruption that is in the World, through Luſt.

O Lord God, add to our Faith Virtue, and to Virtue Knowledge, aud to Knowledge Temperance, and to Temperance Prudence, and to Prudence Patience,

(**14**)

Patience, and to Patience Godlinefs, and to Godlinefs Brotherly Love, and to Brotherly Love, Charity; and grant, O Lord, that Mafonry may be bleft
throughout the World, and thy Peace be upon us,
O Lord; and grant that we may be all united as
one, through our Lord Jefus Chrift, who liveth and
reigneth for ever and ever. *Amen.*

Maf. After you had received this Prayer, what
was faid to you ?

Anf. I was afk'd who I put my Truft in.

Maf. Your Anfwer Brother ?

Anf. In God.

Maf. What was the next Thing faid to you ?

Anf. I was taken by the Right-hand, and he faid,
rife up and follow your Leader, and fear no Danger.

Maf. After all this how was you difpofed of ?

Anf. I was led Three Times round the Lodge.

Maf. Where did you meet with the firft Oppofition ?

Anf. At the Back of the junior Warden in the
South, where I gave the fame three Knocks as at
the Door.

Maf. What Anfwer did he give you ?

Anf. He faid, who comes there.

Maf. Your Anfwer ?

Anf. The fame as at the Door, one who begs to
have and receive, &c.

Maf. Where did you meet with the fecond Oppofition ?

Anf. At the Back of the Senior Warden in
the Weft, where I made the fame Repetition as
at

at the Door. He faid, who comes here? One who begs to have and receive, &c.

Maf. Where did you meet with the third Oppofition?

Anf. At the Back of the Mafter in the Eaft, where I made the Repetition as before.

Maf. What did the Mafter do with you?

Anf. He order'd me back to the Senior Warden in the Weft, to receive Inftructions.

Maf. What was the Inftructions he gave you?

Anf. He taught me to take one Step upon the firft Step of a right Angle oblong Square, with my left Knee bare bent, my Body upright, my right Foot forming a Square, my naked Right-hand upon the Holy Bible, with the Square and Compafs thereon, my Left-hand fupporting the fame; where I took that folemn Obligation or Oath of a Mafon.

Maf. Brother, Can you repeat that Obligation?

Anf. I will do my Endeavour, with your Affiftance, Worfhipful.

Maf. Stand up and begin.

Anf.   I. W------ V------,

Of my own free Will and Accord, on in the Prefence of Almighty God, and this right worfhipful Lodge, dedicated to St. *John*, do hereby and hereon moft folemnly and fincerely fwear, that I will always hail, conceal, and never will reveal any of the fecret Myfteries of Free Mafonry, that fhall be deliver'd to me now, or any Time hereafter, except it be to a true and lawful Brother, or in a juft and lawful Lodge of Brothers and Fellows, him or them whom

(16)

whom I shall find to be such, after just Trial and due Examination.

I furthermore do swear, that I will not write it, print it, cut it, paint it or stint it, mark it, stain it, or engrave it, or cause so be done, upon any Thing moveable or immoveable, under the Canopy of Heaven, whereby it may become legible or intel-legible, or the least Appearance of the Character of a Letter, whereby the secret Art may be unlaw-fully obtain'd. All this I swear, with a strong and steady Resolution to perform the same, without any Hesitation, mental Reservation, or Self-eva-sion of Mind in me whatsoever, under no less Pe-nalty than to have my Throat cut across, my Tongue torn out by the Root, and that to be buried in the Sands of the Sea, at Low-Water Mark, a Cable's Length from the Shore, where the Tide ebbs and flows twice in Twenty-four Hours ; so help me God, and keep me stedfast, in this my enter'd Apprentices Obligation.

[*He kisses the Book.*]

Funde merum Genio.

N. B. After this Obligation they drink a Toast to the Heart that conceals, and to the Tongue that never reveals.

The Master in the Chair gives it, and they all say Ditto, and they draw the Glasses across their Throats as aforesaid.

Maf. Now Brother, after you received this Obli-gation, what was the first that was said to you ?

Anf.

(17)

Anf. I was afk'd what I moft defir'd ?

Maf. What was your Anfwer ?

Anf. To be brought to Light.

Maf. Who brought you to Light ?

Anf. The Mafter and the reft of the Bre-thren.

Maf. When you was thus brought to Light, what were the firft Things you faw ?

Anf. Bible, Square and Compafs.

Maf. What was it they told you they fignified ?

Anf. Three great Lights in Mafonry ?

Maf. Explain them, Brother.

Anf. The Bible, to rule and govern our Faith ; the Square, to Square our Actions ; the Compaffes is to keep us within Bounds with all Men, particularly with a Brother.

Maf. What were the next Things that were fhewn to you ?

Anf. Three Candles, which I was told were Three Leffer Lights in Mafonry.

Maf. What do they reprefent ?

Anf. The Sun, Moon, and Mafter-Mafon.

Maf. Why fo, Brother ?

Anf. There is the Sun to rule the Day, the Moon to rule the Night, and the Mafter-Mafon's Lodge, or at leaft ought fo to do.

Maf. What was then done to you ?

Anf. The Mafter took me by the Right-hand, and gave me the Gripe and Word of

D   an

an enter'd Apprentice, and faid, Rife up Brother Boaz.

N. B. Sometimes they fhew you the Sign before this Gripe and Word is given, which is
Boaz : It is the enter'd Apprentice's Word,
and the Gripe thereto belonging is to pinch
with your Right-thumb Nail, upon the firft
Joint of your Brother's Right-hand.

Maf. Have you got this Gripe and Word,
Brother ?

Anf. I have, Worfhipful

Maf. Give it to your next Brother.

N. B. Then he takes his next Brother by the
Right-hand, and gives him the Gripe and
Word, as before defcribed : he tells the
Mafter, that is right.

According to the following Proof.

The 1*ft*. Brother gives him the Gripe.
The 2*d*. Brother fays, What's this ?
1*ft*. *Bro.* The Gripe of an enter'd Apprentice,
2*d*. *Bro.* Has it got a Name ?
1*ft*. *Bro.* It has.
2*d*. *Bro.* Will you give it me ?
1*ft*. *Bro.* I'll letter it with you, or halve it.
2*d*. *Bro.* I'll halve it with you.
1*ft*. *Bro.* Begin.
2*d*. *Bro.* No, you begin firft.
1*ft*. *Bro.* BO-
2*d*. *Bro.* AZ :
1*ft*. *Bro.* BOAZ.
2*d*. *Bro.* It is right, worfhipful Mafter.

Maf.

(19)

Maſ. What was the next Thing that was ſhewn to you ?

Anſ. The due Guard, or Sign, of an enter'd Apprentice.

N. B. The due Guard or Sign, as they call it, is by drawing your Right-hand a-croſs your Throat edgeways, which is to put you in mind of the Penalty of your Obligation ; that you would ſooner have your Throat cut a-croſs, than diſcover the Secrets of Maſonry : Which I call mere Nonſenſe, and all that peruſe this will ſay the ſame, when they are convinc'd that this is the whole Thing; which they ſoon will find out, only by talking out of this Book to ſome that you know to be Maſons ; but not to let them know that you have read it : You may ſay that you was made at ſome Lodge in the Country, and then ſhew them the Signs and Gripes, and the Words thereunto belonging ; all which are fully deſcrib'd in this Book : Then he will ſoon own you for one of the Fraternity, and take you to his Lodge, as they did me.

Maſ. Have you got that due Guard, or Sign, of an enter'd Apprentice ?

N. B. He draws his Right-hand a-croſs his Throat (as aforeſaid), to ſhew the Maſter that he has.

Maſ. After all this, what was ſaid to you?

Anſ. I was order'd to be taken back, and veſted with what I had been diveſted of ; and to be brought back to return Thanks, and to receive the Benefit of a Lecture, if Time would permit.

D 2   *Maſ.*

Maſ. After you was inveſted of what you had been diveſted of, what was done to you ?

Anſ. I was brought back to the North-weſt Corner of the Lodge, in order to return Thanks.

Maſ. How did you return Thanks ?

Anſ. I ſtood in the North-weſt Corner of the Lodge, and, with the Inſtruction of a Brother, I ſaid, Maſter, ſenior and junior Wardens, ſenior and junior Deacons, and the reſt of the Brethren of this Lodge, I return you Thanks for the Honour you have done me, in making me a Maſon, and admitting me a Member of this worthy Society.

Maſ. What was ſaid to you then ?

Anſ. The Maſter call'd me up to the North-Eaſt Corner of the Lodge, or at his Right-hand.

Maſ. Did he preſent you with any Thing?

Anſ. He preſented me with an Apron, which he put on me ; he told me it was a Badge of Innocency, more antient than the Golden Fleece or the *Roman* Eagle ; more honour'd than the Star and Garter, or any other Order under the Sun, that could be conferr'd upon me at that Time, or any Time hereafter.

Maſ. What were the next Things that were ſhewn to you ?

Anſ. I was ſet down by the Maſter's Right-hand and he ſhew'd me the working Tools of an enter'd Aprentice.

Maſ. What were they ?

Anſ. The 24 Inch Gauge, the Square and common Gavel, or ſetting Maul.

Maſ.

(21)

Maſ. What are their Uſes?

Anſ. The Square to ſquare my Work, the 24 Inch Gauge to meaſure my Work, the common Gavel to knock off all ſuperfluous Matters, whereby the Square may ſet eaſy and juſt.

Maſ. Brother, as we are not all working Maſons, we apply them to our Morals, which we call ſpiritualizing ; explain them.

Anſ. The 24 Inch Gauge repreſents the 24 Hours of the Day.

Maſ. How do you ſpend them Brother ?

Anſ Six Hours to work in, Six Hours to ſerve God, and Six to ſerve a Friend or a Brother, as far as lies in my Power, without being detrimental to myſelf or Family : and Six Hours to Sleep in.

N. B. This is all the enter'd Apprentice's Lecture, which gives the full Deſcription of his making, and is enough for an Apprentice to learn to get Admittance into a Lodge ; but there are ſome fooliſh Reaſons why a Man ſhould be ſerv'd ſo, which I ſhall ſhew you hereafter. But methinks I hear ſome ſay, I am ſurpriz'd that Gentlemen of good Senſe and Reaſon would ſuffer themſelves to be us'd ſo ; to be robb'd of all their Money, and all Manner of Metal, and almoſt ſtrip'd naked, and blinded, with a Halter about his Neck! ſo ſay, I. But the Reaſon is, no Man ever was made a Maſon, but has ſome Friends there that were Maſons already, and perhaps under ſome Obligation, who will ſay, we were ſerv'd ſo before, and were not afraid, but you will hear the Reaſon

Reafon for it all, then you will be fatisfied, and fay our Meaning is good. I myfelf have feen feveral that would not go through it, 'till their Friends have preached the aforefaid Doctrine. I know feveral that have receiv'd the the firft Step, and would go no farther; for there was one Mr. *T*----*s*, a Clergyman, and Curate, of St. *Mary Over*'s, in *Southwark*, fo angry and furpriz'd, that he would have been glad to have made his Efcape from them, provided it had been in his Power; but they would not permit him 'till he had received the Apprentice's Obligations, which they call the firft Pill, that you fhant difcover what you have feen; but when he got away, he never came near them more, and thought himfelf very ill us'd. Two or three more were furpriz'd in that Manner at the fame Lodge, *viz.* at Number II. held then at *T*----*s*, at the Mitre on the *Broad Wall, Chrift Church* in *Surry*, and feveral other Lodges that I have heard of, but this I know to be fact. Alfo the Mafter of a Lodge, who had made a great many Fools, by getting One Pound Five Shillings from each of them: There was half the Money fpent, and the other half kept in the Box for Charitable Ufes; but when they had got to the amount of many Pounds, the Mafter in the Chair, who is fworn moft wickedly not to rob the Lodge, but to ferve it, which he did by carrying it all off, and faid he wanted Charity, therefore he would keep it, and they might do their worft and be d--n'd; and feveral more that I have known to do fuch Tricks, but I don't

(23)

don't care to mention their Names, having said
enough to be underſtood. I think the above
Number confirms the Character; before they
would ſerve a Brother, they would rob him, or
take away his Character, whereby he may loſe
his Buſineſs. I could tell you a great many
bad Things they have done one to another, although they are ſworn ſo bitterly to the contrary: But it would ſwell my Pamphlet into
a large Volume: Therefore I ſhall ſay no
more, becauſe I would not be too ſevere; tho
I have ſaid enough to diſplay their Villainy,
which I hope will be a Caution to all others.

I ſhall now proceed to the Apprentices
Reaſons, as I promis'd you.

THE

Enter'd Apprentice's REASONS.

Maſ. WHY was you neither naked nor
cloath'd, bare-foot nor ſhod, with
a Cable-tow (or Halter) about your Neck?

Anſ. If I had recanted, and ran out in the
Street, the People would have ſaid I was mad;
but if a Brother had ſeen me, he would have
brought me back, and ſeen me done Juſtice
by.

N. B. What a fooliſh Reaſon is this, for Men
of Underſtanding to diſpute about!

Maſ.

(24)

Maſ. Why was you hoodwink'd ?

Anſ. That my Heart might conceal, before my Eyes did diſcover ?

Maſ. The ſecond Reaſon, Brother ?

Anſ. As I was in Darkneſs at that Time, I ſhould keep all the World in Darkneſs.

Maſ. Why was you depriv'd of all Metal.

Anſ. That I ſhould bring nothing offenſive, or defenſive into the Lodge.

Maſ. Give me the third Reaſon, Brother ?

Anſ. As I was poor and pennyleſs when I was made a Maſon, it inform'd me that I ſhould aſſiſt all poor and pennyleſs Brethren, as far as lay in my Power.

Maſ. Brother, you told me you gave Three diſtinct Knocks at the Door : Pray what do they ſignify ?

Anſ. A certain text in Scripture.

Maſ. What is that Text, Brother ?

Anſ. Aſk, and you ſhall have ; ſeek, and you ſhall find ; knock, and it ſhall be opened unto you.

Maſ. How do you apply this Text in Maſonry ?

Anſ. I ſought in my Mind ; I aſk'd of my Friend ; I knock'd, and the Door of Maſonry became open unto me.

Maſ. Why had you a Sword, Spear, or ſome other warlike Inſtrument, preſented to your naked Left-breaſt particularly ?

Anſ. Becauſe the Left-breaſt is the neareſt the Heart, that it might be the more a Prick

to

29

(**25**)

to my Confcience as it prick'd my flefh at that Time.

Maf. Why was you led three Times round the Lodge ?

Anf. That all the Brethren might fee I was duly prepar'd.

Maf. When you was made an Apprentice, why was your Left-knee bare bent.

Anf. Becaufe the Left-knee is the weakeft Part of my Body, and an enter'd Apprentice is the weakeft Part of Mafonry, which I was then entering into.

N. B. There are fome more Reafons, but they are fo foolifh that they are not worth mentioning ; fo I fhall proceed to the Form of the Lodge, as follows.

XXXXXXXXXXXXXXXXXXXXXX

The Form of a L O D G E.

Maf. BROTHER, we have been talking a great while about a Lodge ; Pray what makes a Lodge ?

Anf. A certain Number of Mafons met to-gether to work.

Maf. Pray what Number makes a Lodge ?
Anf. Three, Five, Seven, or Eleven.

Maf. Why do Three make a Lodge, Bro-ther ?

Anf. Becaufe there were three Grand Ma-fons in the building of the World, and alfo

E   that

(26)

that noble Piece of Architecture Man ; which
are so complete in Proportion, that the Anti-
ents began their Architecture by the same
Rules.

Maf. The second Reason, Brother ?

Anf. There were three Grand Masons at
the building of *Solomon*'s Temple.

Maf. Why do Five make a Lodge ?

Anf. Because every Man is endued with Five
Senses.

Maf. What are the Five Senses ?

Anf. Hearing, Seeing, Smelling, Tasting,
and Feeling.

Maf. What Use are those Five Senses to
you, in Masonry ?

Anf. Three are of great Use to me, *viz.*
Hearing, Seeing, and Feeling.

Maf. What Use are they, Brother ?

Anf. Hearing, is to hear the Word; Seeing, is to see the Sign ; Feeling, is to feel
the Gripe ; that I may know a Brother, as
well in the Dark as in the Light.

Maf. Why should Seven make a Lodge ?
Anf. Because there are Seven liberal Sciences.

Maf. Will you name them, Brother ?

Anf. Grammar, Rhetoric, Logic, Arithmetic, Geometry, Music, and Astronomy.

Maf. What do those Sciences teach you ?

Anf. Grammar teaches me the Art of writing and speaking the Language, wherein I
learn according to the First, Second, and Third
Concord.

Maf.

(27)

Maf. What doth Rhetoric teach you?

Anf. The Art of fpeaking and difcourfing upon any Topic whatfoever.

Maf. What doth Logic teach you?

Anf. The Art of reafoning well, whereby you may find out Truth from Falfhood.

Maf. What doth Arithmetic teach you?

Anf. The Virtue of Numbers.

Maf. What doth Geometry teach you?

Anf. The Art of meafuring, whereby the *Egyptians* found out their own Land, or the fame Quantity which they had before the overflowing of the River *Nile*, which frequently us'd to flow to water their Country; at which Time they fled to the Mountains till it went off again, which made them have continual Quarrels about their Lands; for every Man thought he was robb'd, and had not his Right, till *Euclid* found out Geometry, and meafur'd every Man his Due, and gave them Plans of each Man's Ground, with the juft Quantity that belong'd to him; then they were all fatisfied; and the fame Rule is continu'd in all Nations to this Day.

Maf. What doth Mufic teach you, Brother?

Anf. The Virtue of Sounds.

Maf. What doth Aftronomy teach you?

Anf. The Knowledge of the heavenly Bodies.

N. B. See *Brandt's* Aftronomical Tables, and you will have a full Defcription of the laft Science. But I believe you may content yourfelf without any other Authors upon

E 2   this

(28)

this Head, for I go as far as any of the Free Mafons do in their Lectures, and rather further, which I am obliged to do to make it plain, that it may be underftood to the meaneft Capacity. That which is not in the Lecture is marked thus, *N. B.*

Maf. Why fhould Eleven make a Lodge, Brother ?

Anf. There were Eleven *Patriarchs,* when *Jofeph* was fold into *Egypt,* and fuppos'd to be loft.

Maf. The Second Reafon, Brother ?

Anf. There were but Eleven Apoftles when *Judas* had betray'd Chrift.

Maf. What Form is your Lodge ?
Anf. An Oblong Square.

Maf. How long, Brother ?
Anf. From Eaft to Weft.

Maf. How wide, Brother ?
Anf. Between North and South.

Maf. How high, Brother ?
Anf. From the Earth to the Heavens.

Maf. How deep, Brother ?
Anf. From the Surface of the Earth to the Center,

Maf. Why is your Lodge faid to be from the Surface to the Center of the Earth ?

Anf. Becaufe that Mafonry is Univerfal.

Maf. Why is your Lodge fituated Eaft and Weft ?

Anf. Becaufe all Churches and Chapels are, or ought to be fo,.

Maf.

Maf. Why fo, Brother ?

Anf. Becaufe the Gofpel was firft preached in the Eaft, and extended itfelf to the Weft.

Maf. What fupports your Lodge ?

Anf. Three great Pillars.

Maf. What are their Names ?

Anf. Wifdom, Strength and Beauty.

Maf. Who doth the Pillar of Wifdom reprefent ?

Anf. The Mafter in the Eaft.

Maf. Who doth the Pillar of Strength reprefent ?

Anf. The Senior Warden in the Weft.

Maf. Who doth the Pillar of Beauty reprefent ?

Anf. The Junior Warden in the South.

Maf. Why fhould the Mafter reprefent the Pillar of Wifdom ?

Anf. Becaufe he gives Inftructions to the Crafts to carry on their Work in a proper Manner, with good Harmony.

Maf. Why fhould the Senior Warden reprefent the Pillar of Strength ?

Anf. As the Sun fets to finifh the Day, fo the Senior Warden ftands in the Weft to pay the Hirelings their Wages ; which is the Strength and Support of all Bufinefs.

Maf. Why fhould the Junior Warden reprefent the Pillar of Beauty ?

Anf. Becaufe he ftands in the South, at high Twelve at Noon, which is the Beauty of the Day, to call the Men off from Work to Refrefhment, and to fee that they come on again

in

Samuel Pritchard

(30)

in due Time, that the Master may have Pleasure and Profit therein.

Maſ. Why is it ſaid that your Lodge is supported by theſe Three great Pillars, Wiſdom, Strength and Beauty?

Anſ. Becauſe Wiſdom, Strength and Beauty is the Finiſher of all Works, and nothing can be carried on without them.

Maſ. Why ſo, Brother?

Anſ. Becauſe there is Wiſdom to contrive, Strength to ſupport, and Beauty to adorn.

Maſ. Had you any Covering to your Lodge?

Anſ. Yes, a cloudy Canopy, of divers Colours, or the Clouds.

Maſ. How blows a Maſon's Wind, Brother?

Anſ. Due Eaſt and Weſt.

Maſ. What is it o' Clock, Brother?
Anſ. High Twelve.

Maſ. Call the Men off from Work to Refreſhment, and ſee that they come on again in due Time.

[*The End of the enter'd Apprentice's Lecture.*]

The

(81)

The enter'd Apprentice's Song, which is sung after grave Business is done, or after making a Brother.

I.

COME let us prepare,
   We *Brothers* that are,
Assembled on merry Occasion ;
   Let's drink, laugh, and sing ;
   Our Wine has a Spring ;
Here's a Health to an *Accepted Mason.*

II.

The World is in pain
Our *Secrets* to gain,
And still let them wonder and gaze on ;
   They ne'er can divine
   The *Word* or the *Sign*
Of a *Free* and *Accepted Mason.*

III.

'Tis *This*, and 'tis *That*,
They cannot tell *What*,
Why so many *Great Men* of the Nation
   Should *Aprons* put on,
   To make themselves one
With a *Free* and an *Accepted Mason.*

IV.

Great *Kings*, *Dukes* and *Lords*,
Have laid by their Swords,
Our *Myst'ry* to put a good Grace on,
   And ne'er been asham'd
   To hear themselves nam'd
With a *Free* and an *Accepted Mason.*

V. An-

36

32

V.

Antiquity's Pride
We have on our Side,
And it maketh Men juft in their Station :
There's nought but what's Good,
To be underftood
By a *Free* and an *Accepted Mafon.*

VI.

We're true and fincere,
And juft to the *Fair,*
Who will truft us on ev'ry Occafion ;
No Mortals can more
The *Ladies* adore,
Than a *Free* and an *Accepted Mafon.*

VII.

Then join *Hand* in *Hand,*
T' each other firm ftand,
Let's be merry, and put a bright Face on :
What Mortal can boaft
So *Noble a Toaft,*
As a *Free* and an *Accepted Mafon.*

VIII.

W'ere true and fincere,
And juft to the *Fair,*
Who will truft us on ev'ry Occafion ;
No Mortal can more,
The Ladies adore,
Than a *Free* and an *Accepted Mafon.*

N. B. When they fing the aforefaid Song,
they all ftand round a great Table, and join
Hands a-crofs, that is, your Right-hand takes
hold

hold of your Left-hand Man's Left-hand; and your Left-hand Man, with his Right-hand, takes hold of his left Man's Left-hand, and fo croffing all round. But when they fay the laft Verfe, they jump up all together, ready to fhake the Floor down: I myfelf have been below, where there has been a Lodge, and have heard the People fay, L—d d---mn their Bloods, what are they doing? They will fhake the Place down, I'll ftay here no longer. This they call driving of Piles, to amufe the world; but they fhall not be amus'd any longer, but fhall know every particular, and the foolifh Reafons they give for them.

How they call off the Men from Work to Refrefhment.

THE Mafter whifpers to the fenior Deacon at his Right-hand, and fays, 'tis my Will and Pleafure that this Lodge is called off from Work to Refrefhment during Pleafure ; then the fenior Deacon carries it to the junior War-den, and whifpers the fame Words in his Ear, and he whifpers it in the Ear of the junior Deacon at his Right-hand, and he carries it to the junior Warden, and whifpers the fame to him, who declares it with a loud Voice, and fays, it is our Mafter's Will and Pleafure, that this Lodge is called from Work to Refrefh-ment, during Pleafure ; then he fets up his Column, and the Senior lays his down ; for the

F   Care

(34)

Care of the Lodge is in the Hands of the junior Warden, while they are at Refreshment.

N. B. The senior and junior Warden have each of them a Column in their Hand, about Twenty Inches long, which represents the Two Columns of the Porch at *Solomon's* Temple, BOAZ and JACHIN. *

The Senior is BOAZ, or Strength.
The Junior is JACHIN, or to establish.

* Vide 1 Kings, Chap. vii.

_____

How to call on to Work again.

IT is the same as calling off from Work, only with this Difference ; it is our Master's Will and Pleasure that this Lodge is called off from Refreshment to Work; then the Junior lays down his Column, and the senior Warden sets up his ; so they proceed to a Lecture, which they call Work.

N. B. If time does not permit for the Craft's Lecture, as it very seldom does, having gone through the aforesaid Lecture, then they close the Lodge ; which is much the same as opening, only with this Difference ; the senior Warden declares it, and says,

It is our Master's Will and Pleasure, that this Lodge stands clos'd till the first, or third *Wednesday* in the next Month (or according to
the

(35)

the Nights that their Lodge is held on), except a Lodge of Emergency, and that you
fhall have timely Notice of ; then they take off
their Jewels, and get as drunk as Free-mafons
may be ; and fing and get drunk, and that's all.

The *FELLOW-CRAFT's Part.*

Maf. BROTHER, are you a Fellow-
 Craft ?

Anf. I am ; try me, prove me.

Maf. Where was you made a Craft ?

Anf. In a juft and lawful Lodge of Crafts.

Maf. How was you prepar'd to be made a
Craft ?

Anf. I was neither naked not cloath'd, bare-
foot nor fhod ; in a halting moving Pofture,
depriv'd of all Metal, I was led to the Door of
he Lodge by the Hand of a Brother.

Maf. How got you admittance ?

Anf. By Three diftinct Knocks.

Maf. What was faid to you within ?

Anf. Who comes there.

Maf. Your Anfwer, Brother?

Anf. One who hath ferv'd his Time juftly
and lawfully as an enter'd Apprentice, and now
begs to become more perfect in Mafonry, by
being admitted a Fellow-Craft.

F 2

Maf.

(36)

Maſ. How do you expect to attain it ?
Anſ. By the Benefit of a Paſs-word:

Maſ. Have you got that Paſs-word ?
Anſ. I have.

Maſ. Give it me ?
Anſ. SHIBBOLETH.*

Maſ. What did he ſay to you then ?
Anſ. Paſs, Shibboleth.

Maſ. What became of you then ?
Anſ. I was led twice round the Lodge.

Maſ. Where did you meet with the firſt Oppoſition ?
Anſ. At the Back of the ſenior Warden, where I made the ſame Repetition as at the Door.

Maſ. Where did you meet with the ſecond Oppoſition ?
Anſ. At the Back of the Maſter, where I made the ſame Repetition as at the Door.

Maſ. What did he do with you ?
Anſ. He order'd me back to the ſenior Warden, to receive Inſtruction.

Maſ. What Inſtructions did he give you ?
Anſ. He taught me to ſhew the Maſter my due Guard, and to take Two Steps upon the ſecond Step of a right-angl'd oblong Square, with my Right-knee bent bare, my Left-foot forming a Square, my Body upright, my Right-hand upon the holy Bible, my Left-arm ſupported by the Point of the Compaſſes, forming a Square ; where I took the Obligation of a Fellow-Craft.

* Vide Judges, Chap. xii.

Maſ.

(**37**)

Maſ. Have you got that Obligation, Brother?
Anſ. I have, Worſhipful.

Maſ. Will you repeat it, Brother ?
Anſ. I'll do my Endeavour, with your Aſſiſt nce, Worſhipful.

Maſ. Stand up and begin.
Anſ.   I W----- V------,

Of my own Will and Accord, and in the Preſence of Almighty God and this right worſhipful Lodge, dedicated to St. *John*, do hereby, and hereon, moſt ſolemnly and ſincerely ſwear, that I will always hail, conceal, and never will reveal that Part of a Fellow-Craft to an enter'd Apprentice, or either of them, except it be in a true and lawful Lodge of Crafts, him or them, whom I ſhall find to be ſuch after juſt Trial and due Examination.

I furthermore do ſwear, that I will anſwer all Signs and Summonſes ſent to me from a Lodge of Crafts, within the Length of my Cable-Tow.

I alſo ſwear, that I will not wrong a Brother, or ſee him wrong'd, but give him timely Notice of all approaching Dangers whatſoever, as far as my Knowledge leads me. I will alſo ſerve a Brother as far as lies in my Power, without being detrimental to myſelf or Family ; and I will keep all my Brother's Secrets as my own, that ſhall be delivered to me as ſuch, Murder and Treaſon only excepted.

And that at my own free Will, all this I ſwear, with a firm and ſteady Reſolution to perform the ſame, without any Equivocation

or

(38)

or Hesitation in me whatsoever, under no less
Penalty than to have my Heart torn from un-
der my naked Left-breast, and given to the
Vultures of the Air as a Prey: So help me
God, and keep me stedfast in this my Craft's
Obligation.

[*He kisses the Book.*]

N. B. The Length of the Cable-Tow is
Three Miles; therefore if a Brother is Three
Miles from his Lodge, he is clear of all Fines,
and of this Obligation; for it saith within the
Length of my Cable-Tow.

Maf. After you receiv'd this Obligation,
what was shewn to you?
Anf. The Sign of a Fellow-Craft.

N. B. This Sign is by putting your Right-
hand to your Left-breast, and keeping your
Thumb square, and your Left-hand upright,
forming a Square.

Maf. What was next done to you?
Anf. He took me by the Right-hand and
gave me the Gripe and Word of a Fellow-
Craft and Pass-Gripe.

N. B. The Pass-Gripe is by putting your
Thumb-nail between the first and second
Joint of the Right-hand, and the Word is
Shibboleth. The Craft's Gripe is on the se-
cond Joint of the aforesaid Hand, and the
Word is *Jachin.*

Maf. What did he then do to you?
Anf. He took me by the Right-hand, and
said, rise up Brother *Jachin.*

Maf.

(39)

Maſ. What did he do then to you ?

Anſ. He order'd me back, and to be inveſt-ed of what I had been diveſted of, and brought back in order to return Thanks.

N. B. He returns Thanks in the ſame Man-ner as the Apprentice, only with this Differ-ence, for admitting a Fellow-Craft.

Maſ. After you was thus admitted a Fel-low-Craft, did you ever work as a Craft ?
Anſ. Yes in the Building of the Temple.

Maſ. Where did you receive your Wages?
Anſ. In the Middle Chamber.

Maſ. When you came to the Door of the Middle Chamber, who did you ſee ?
Anſ. A Warden.

Maſ. What did he demand of you ?
Anſ. The Paſs-word of a Craft.

Maſ. did you give it him ?
Anſ. I did.

Maſ. What is it ?
Anſ. SHIBBOLETH.

Maſ. How got you to the Middle Chamber?
Anſ. Through the Porch.

Maſ. Did you ſee any Thing worth your Notice ?
Anſ. I did.

Maſ. What was it ?
Anſ. Two fine Braſs Pillars.

Maſ. What were they call'd ?
Anſ. BOAZ and JACHIN.

Maſ.

(40)

Maſ. How high were theſe Pillars ?

Anſ. Thirty-five Cubits, with a Chapiter Five Cubits, which makes it Forty high.*

N. B. In the firſt of *Kings*, Chap. vii. Ver. 20, it ſays, They were but 18 Cubits high, and a Line of 12 Cubits meaſured them round; that is, about 4 Cubits Diameter, which is greatly out of Proportion according to all Orders that ever were or ever will be ; as any muſt ſay, that underſtands Architecture, for it is not quite four Diameters and an half, which is too ſhort by four Diameters at leaſt ; for if they were in the *Dorick* Order, they ſhould be eight Diameters. Therefore, how thick and clumſy they muſt look, to be but half the Height they ſhould be, or a little better. As for Example, ſuppoſe the Monument upon *Fiſh-ſtreet-bill*, which is after the *Dorick* Order, was but half the Height, and the ſame Diameter, how would it look ? very thick and clumſy, like as it were all of a Lump.
But this can't be the Thing with theſe two Columns, for it is plain that *Solomon*'s Temple was a grand Building, and every Thing in Proportion, and it anſwers exactly with the *Corinthian* or Compoſite Order, for it is ten Diameters high, or thereabouts ; and it is ſaid in Chap. iii. Ver. 15, of the Second Book of *Chronicles*, 35 Cubits high, and the Chapiters 5 Cubits each, which makes 40 Cubits ; the Diameter 4 Cubits, and the aforeſaid Order is 10 Diameters high, that is, 4 Times is 40, which

* Vide 2 Chron. Chap. iii. Ver. 15.

(41)

which is juſt 60 Feet high of our *Engliſh* Meaſure*.

Ma What were they adorned with Brother?'
Anſ. Two Chapiters, Five Cubits high each.

Maſ. What elſe were they adorned with?
Anſ. Net-work, Lillywork and Pomegranates.

Maſ. Were they hollow, Brother?
Anſ. They were hollow.

Maſ. How thick was the Rhind or Shell?
Anſ. Four Inches, or a Hand's Breadth.

Maſ. Where were they caſt?
Anſ. On the Plain of *Jordan*, in Clay Ground, between *Succoth* and *Zartha*, where the reſt of *Solomon*'s holy Veſſels were caſt.

Maſ. Who caſt them?
Anſ. Hiram Abiff, the Widow's Son.

N. B. Some Maſters of Lodges will argue upon Reaſons about the holy Veſſels in the Temple, and the Windows and Doors, the Length, Breadth and Height of every Thing in the Temple. Saying, why was it ſo and ſo? One will give one Reaſon, and another will give another Reaſon, and thus they will continue for two or three Hours in this Part and the Maſter-Part; but this happens but very ſeldom, except an *Iriſhman* ſhould come, who likes to hear himſelf talk, aſking, why were they round?

G   Why

* There are Three Sorts of Cubits, viz. the King's Cubit, Three Feet Engliſh Meaſure; the holy Cubit, One Foot Six Inches; the common Cubit, One Foot Nine Inches: Therefore, whenever you read of the Word Cubit in the Bible, it is One Foot Six Inches.

(42)

Why were they fquare? Why were they hollow? Why were the Stones coftly? Why were they hewn Stones and faw'd Stones, &c. fome give one Reafon and fome give another; thus you fee that every Man's Reafon is not alike. Therefore, if I give you my Reafon, it may not be like another; but any Man that reads the foregoing and following Work, and confults the 5th, 6th, 7th and 8th Chapters of the firft Book of *Kings*, and the 2d, 3d and 4th of the fecond Book of *Chronicles*, may reafon as well as the beft of them; for I have laid all the Rules down plain to go by.

[*The End of the Fellow-Crafts Part.*]

The FELLOW-CRAFTS Song.

I.

HAIL Masonry? Thou *Craft* divine?
   Glory of Earth, from Heaven reveal'd;
Which do'ft with Jewels precious fhine,
   From all but Mafons Eyes conceal'd.

CHORUS.

Thy Praifes due who can rehearfe,
In nervons Profe, or flowing Verfe.

II.

As Men from Brutes diftinguifh'd are,
   A *Mafon* other Men excels;
For what's in Knowledge choice and rare
   But in his Breaft fecurely dwells?

CHORUS.

(43)

CHORUS.

His silent Breast and faithful Heart
Preserves the Secrets of the Art.

III.

From scorching Heat, and piercing Cold ;
    From Beasts, whose Roar the Forest rends ;
From the Assaults of Warriors bold
    The Masons Art Mankind defends.

CHORUS.

Be to this Art due Honour paid,
From which Mankind receives such Aid.

IV.

Ensigns of State, that feed our Pride,
    Distinctions troublesome and vain !
By *Masons* true are laid aside :
    Arts free-born *Sons* such Toys disdain ;

CHORUS.

Ennobled by the Name they bear,
Distinguish'd by the Badge they wear.

V.

Sweet Fellowship, from Envy free :
    Friendly Converse of Brotherhood ;
The *Lodge*'s lasting Cement be !
    Which has for Ages firmly stood.

CHORUS.

A Lodge, thus built for Ages past.
Has lasted, and will ever last.

G 2   VI. Then

(44)

VI.

Then in our Songs be Juſtice done
  To thoſe who have enrich'd the *Art*,
From *Jabal* down to *Burlington*,
  And let each Brother bear a Part.

CHORUS.

Let noble Maſons *Healths go round*;
Their Praiſe in lofty Lodge *reſound*.

N. B. The Fellow-Craft's Clap is by forming the Craft's Sign, *i. e.* by holding your
Left-hand up, keeping it ſquare; then clap
with your Right-hand and Left together, and
from thence ſtrike your Left-Breaſt with your
Right-hand; then ſtrike your Apron, and
your Right-foot going at the ſame Time.
This is done altogether as one Clap, or at leaſt
ſhould be, which makes a great Shaking on
the Floor, and. what they call driving of Piles
to amuſe the World; but they ſhall not be a-
muſed any longer, but ſhall have the Truth.
Nay, I have known ſome Lodges that have
had Shores ſet below to ſupport the Floor,
while they have been at work as they call it.

How

(45)

How to discover a Mason by drinking with him in Company, and what Degree of Masonry he has past, and none of the Company can discover it but Masons.

IF he takes his Pot or Glass, and draws it a-cross his Throat before he drinks or after, then he is an Apprentice, because that is the Penalty of his Obligation: that he would have his Throat cut a-cross before he would discover any thing of Masonry.

Or, if he draws it a-cross his Left-breast, touching the same, he is a Craft, for that is the Penalty of the Craft's Obligation, *i. e.* He would sooner have his Heart torn from under his naked Left-breast, and given to the Vultures of the Air as a Prey, than discover any Part of Masonry.

Or, if he draws it a-cross his Belly, he is a Master, for that is the Penalty of the Master's Obligation; *i. e.* He would sooner have his Body sever'd in two; one Part carried to the South and the other to the North, his Bowels burnt to Ashes in the South, than he would discover any Part of Masonry.

N. B. He may do the same with his naked Right-hand as with a Pot or Glass, but it is less taken notice of with a Pot or Glass than with your Hand.

But in the Lodge they always drink out of Glasses, and put them down as it is said in the Apprentices Part; but it it is a Lodge of all Master Masons, before they set the Glass down upon the Table where they all sit round, as
afore-

(46)

aforefaid, they draw it a-crofs their Throat, from thence a-crofs their Left-breaft, touching the fame, from thence a-crofs their Belly, and then making three Motions to fet it down, at the Third fet it down altogether ; the Mafter gives the Word, faying, Here goes one, two and three, fetting it down ; but if it is a Craft's Lodge, they draw it twice a-crofs their Throats and once to their Breaft ; and if it is an Apprentice's Lodge, they draw it three Times a-crofs their Throats, and fets it down at the third Motion, as aforefaid.

Thus they will many Times continue exercifing till Morning, though their Family want them at home. Come, they will fay, let us have the other Fire, then we will go ! Says another, we can't, for our Bowl is out ! Then fays another, let's have it fill'd again ! This has been the Ruin of Mafonry, which was far from the firft Defign of it ; but Liquor makes Men forget that they are Men, and makes all good things become corrupted and bad.

Cura fugit multo diluiturque mero
Tunc Dolor & Curæ rugaque Frontis abeft.

Full Bowls, or chafe, or elfe diffolve our Cares, ⎫
Then far away are banifh'd Griefs and Fears, ⎬
Nor thoughtful Wrinkle in the Face appears. ⎭

Thus, a great many People think that it is a great Service for a Man to be made a Mafon ; fo it is, to be his Ruin ; and when he is in the greateft Diftrefs they will talk againft him, becaufe he can't pay what they demand. I can't fay that I ever knew any Mafon of late Years,

get

get any Thing by going to Lodges, without it
is a Publican that keeps the Houfe. Although
they are fworn to ferve a Brother, I never knew
they did, but hurt him. I have known Mafons
to arreft a Brother, fummon a Brother to
the Court of Requeft, and feize a Brother's
Goods, for lefs than Twenty Shillings. I have
likewife known them put a Brother In Goal,
and do him a great deal more Mifchief, which
I don't care to fpeak too plain to their Confciences, which I am in hopes to foften ; for when
it has been in their power to ferve a Brother,
they have, at the fame Time, endeavoured to
ruin him. Therefore, I hope this will be a
Warning to all honeft Men to keep from thefe
Oaths, without they intend to perform them,
for they are very folemn.

I think I have heard fome fay, it is furpriz-
ing that they all fhould be bad ! No,
God forbid they fhould, but I will tell you the
Reafon why they are fo.

There are a great many good Men, Members of Lodges, that little think of the Villainy that is carried on among fome of them ;
but when he finds them out, he'll leave the
Lodge, and be no more concerned with them,
but he will not tell his Reafons to the World ;
if he did, he would be forfworn. I have
known fome young Brethren to have found
them out a little after they were made, and
have left the Lodge upon that Account. This
is the Reafon that they act fo contrary to their
Obligation, becaufe honeft Men can't bear it
long, fo the Scum of the Earth are left to be
Mafters of Lodges.

The

(48)

✻✻✻✻✻✻✻✻✻✻✻✻✻✻✻✻✻✻✻✻✻✻✻✻

The M A S T E R's PART.

Maſ. WHERE have you been, Brother ?
   Anſ. I have been to the Weſt,

 Maſ. And where are you going ?
Anſ. To the Eaſt.

 Maſ. What makes you leave the Weſt and go to the Eaſt ?
 Anſ. Becauſe the Light of the Goſpel was firſt ſhewn in the Eaſt.

 Maſ. What are you going to do in the Eaſt, Brother ?
 Anſ. To ſeek for a Lodge of Maſters.

 Maſ. Then I preſume you are a Maſter Maſon, Brother ?
 Anſ. I am ſo taken amongſt Maſters.

 Maſ. Where was you paſt Maſter ?
 Anſ. In a Lodge of Maſters.

 Maſ. How was you prepar'd to be made a Maſter ?
 Anſ. I had my Shoes taken from off my Feet, both my Arms and Breaſt naked, depriv'd of all Metal. I was led to the Door of the Lodge.

 N. B. In the Craft's Part, the Right-breaſt is naked, and the Right-ſhoe off, and in the Apprentices Part, the Left-arm and Left-breaſt is naked, with the Left-ſhoe off, and the Maſter's Part, as aforeſaid in the Lecture.

          Maſ.

(49)

Maſ. How got you Admittance ?

Anſ. By Three diſtinct Knocks.

Maſ. What was ſaid to you then within ?

Anſ. Who comes there ?

Maſ. Your Anſwer, Brother ?

Anſ. One who hath juſtly and lawfully ſerved his Time as an Enter'd Apprentice, and ſome Time Fellow-Craft, now begs to become more perfect in Maſonry to be made a Maſter.

Maſ. How do you expect to attain it ?

Anſ. By the Benefit of a Paſs-word.

Maſ. Will you give me that Paſs-word ?

Anſ. I will.

Maſ. Give it me then.

Anſ. TUBAL-CAIN.

Maſ. What was ſaid to you then ?

Anſ. Enter TUBAL-CAIN.

Maſ. How was you dispos'd of ?

Anſ. I was led once round the Lodge.

Maſ. Where did you meet with the firſt Oppoſition ?

Anſ. At the Back of the Maſter.

Maſ. What did he demand of you ?

Anſ. The ſame as at the Door.

Maſ. How did he diſpoſe of you ?

Anſ. He order'd me back to the ſenior Warden in the Weſt to receive Inſtructions.

Maſ. What were the Inſtructions you received of the ſenior Warden ?

Anſ. He taught me as I ſtood in the Weſt to ſhew the Maſter in the Eaſt my due Guard or Sign of an Apprentice, and to take one

H   Step

(50)

Step upon the First Step of the Right-Angle Oblong Square, my other Foot forming a Square.

Secondly, I was taught to take two Steps upon the same Oblong Square, shewing him the Sign of a Fellow-Craft.

Thirdly, I was taught to take Three Steps upon the same Oblong Square, with both my Knees bent bare, my Body upright, my Right-hand upon the Holy Bible, both the Points of the Compasses extended to my Right and Left-breast, where I took that solemn Obligation or Oath of a Master Mason.

Mas. Can you repeat the Obligation you speak of?

Ans. I'll do my Endeavour, Worshipful, with your Assistance.

Mas. Stand up and begin, Brother.

Ans.   I. W—— V——,

Of my own free Will and Accord, and in the Presence of Almighty God, and this right worshipful Lodge, dedicated to St. *John*, do hereby and hereon most solemnly and sincerely swear, that I will always hail, conceal, and never will reveal, that Part of a Master Mason to a Fellow-Craft, no more than that of a Fellow Craft to an enter'd Apprentice, or any of them to the rest of the World , except it be to a true and lawful Lodge of Masters, him, or them, whom I shall find to be such, after just Trial and due Examination.

I further-

(51)

I furthermore do fwear, that I will anfwer all Signs and Summonfes, fent to me from a Lodge of Mafters, within the length of my Cable-tow.

I alfo will keep all my Brother's Secrets as my own, that is delivered to me as fuch, Murder and Treafon only excepted, and that at my own free Will: I will not wrong a Brother or fee him wrong'd, but give him timely Notice of all approaching Dangers, as far as my Knowledge leads me.

I alfo will ferve a Brother as far as lies in my Power, without being detrimental to my-felf or Family.

And I furthermore do promife, that I will not have any carnal Converfation with a Bro-ther's Wife, Sifter or Daughter, and that I will never difcover what is done in the Lodge, but that I will be agreeable to all Laws what-foever. All this I fwear, with a firm and fteady Refolution to perform the fame, with-out any Hefitation in me whatfoever, under no lefs Penalty than to have my Body fever'd in two, the one Part carried to the South, and the other to the North; my Bowels burnt to Afhes in the South, and the Afhes to be fcatter'd before the Four Winds, that fuch a vile Wretch as I fhould be remember'd no more amongft any Manner of Men, (particu-larly Mafons) fo help me God, and keep me ftedfaft in this my Mafter's Obligation.

[*He kiffes the Book.*]

Maf. What was fhewn to you after you had received this Obligation?

H 2
Anf.

Anf. One of the Mafter's Signs.

N. B. It is by drawing your Right-hand edge-ways acrofs your Belly, which is the Pe-nalty of your Mafter's Obligation. He takes you then by the Apprentices Gripe, and fays, what's this ? You fay the Gripe of an enter'd Apprentice.

Maf. Has it got a Name ?
Anf. It has.

Maf. Will you give it me ?
Anf. Boaz.

Maf. Will you be of or from ?
Anf. From.

Maf. From what, Brother ?
Anf. From an enter'd Apprentice to a Fel-low-Craft.

Maf. Pafs Brother.

N. B. Then he puts his Thumb between the Firft and Second Joint, which is the Pafs Gripe, and you fay Shibboleth.

Maf. What was done to you then ?
Anf. He took me by the Gripe of a Fellow-Craft, and faid what is this?

Maf. Your Anfwer, Brother ?
Anf. The Gripe of a Fellow-Craft.

Maf. Has it got a Name ?
Anf. It has.

Maf. Will you give it me ?
Anf. Jachin.

Maf. What was faid to you then ?

Anf.

(**53**)

Anf. Rife up Brother JACHIN, Obligated Mafter.

Maf. What was faid to you then, Brother?

Anf. He told me I then reprefented one of the greateft Men in the World, our grand Mafter *Hiram*, who was killed juft at the Finifhing of the firft Temple, as you fhall hear.

There were Fifteen Fellow-Crafts, finding the Temple almoft finifhed, and they had not received the Mafter's Word, becaufe their Time was not come, therefore they agreed to extort them from their Mafter *Hiram* the firft Opportunity, that they might pafs for Mafters in other Countries, and have Mafter's Wages; but twelve of thefe Crafts recanted, and the other three were refolved to carry it on; their Names were *Jubela*, *Jubelo* and *Jubelum*. Thefe three Crafts knowing it was always the Mafter's Cuftom at high Twelve at Noon, when the Men were call'd off to Refrefhment, to go into *Sanctum Sanctorum*, to pray to the true and living God: Thofe three Ruffians placed themfelves at the three Entrances of the Temple, *viz.* The Weft Door, the South Door and Eaft Door.

There was no Entrance in at the North, becaufe the Sun darts no Rays from thence: Thus they waited while he had made his Prayer to the Lord, to have the Word and Gripe as he came out, or his Life; but fome Mafons fay, as he went in. So *Hiram* came to the Eaft Door, and *Jubela* demanded the Mafter's Word: He told him he did not receive it in

fuch

such a Manner; but he must wait, and Time and a little Patience would bring him to it, for it was not in his Power to deliver it alone, except Three together, *viz. Solomon*, King of *Israel*; *Hiram*, King of *Tyre*; and *Hiram Abiff*. He not being satisfied with this Answer, struck him a-cross the Throat with a 24 Inch Gauge: He fled from thence to the South Door, where he thought to have made his Way; but he was accosted in the same Manner by *Jubelo*, to whom he gave the same Answer as the former; but he not being satisfied, gave him a Blow with the Square upon his Left-breast, which made him reel: But having recover'd his Strength, he fled to the West Door, where he thought to have made his Escape; but he was accosted in the same Manner, as at the two other Doors, by *Jubelum*, to whom he made the same Reply as before; but he not being satisfied therewith, gave him a greater Blow than either of the former, with a common Gavel, or Setting Maul, upon his Head, which prov'd his Death. After this they carry'd him out at the West Door, and hid him in a Heap of Rubbish till high Twelve at Night, when they found Means to bury him on the Side of a Hill, in a handsome Grave, Six Foot East and West, and Six Foot perpendicular.

N. B. Some Masons say that he was not carry'd out at the West Door, but was bury'd in the Place where he was killed.

They hold that the Three Ruffians took up a Stone in the Temple, and made a Hole and put him in, and cover'd him over with the

Stone,

Stone, and carry'd the Rubbish out in their Aprons; but which it is I can't say, nor come at the exact Truth: For some Masons say he was carry'd out, and some say not; so I leave it to them to determine.

Maf. After you was thus knock'd down, what was said to you then?

Anf. He said I represented one of the greatest Men in the World, our Grand-Master *Hiram*, lying dead.

N. B. The junior Warden struck you with a 24 Inch Gauge, a-cross your Throat; the senior Warden struck you with the Square, upon your Left-breast; and the Master struck you upon the Head and kill'd you: So you are laid down upon the Floor on your Back, suppos'd to be dead, tho' you are not hurt; But only to represent the Death of your Master *Hiram*.

The *French* have a very solemn Way of representing his Death; for when you come into the Lodge to be made a Master, there is a Brother laid down in the Place where you are to-lie, with his Face all besmear'd with Blood; and they say to you, Brother don't be frighten-en'd, for one of our Brother's is kill'd because he would not deliver the Master's Word and Gripe to the Three Fellow-Crafts, that had no Right to it; and it is the Duty of us all so to do, to die before we will deliver any Part of Masonry to them that have no Right to it.

When you kneel down to receive the Obli-gation, the suppos'd dead Man lies behind you; and while you are reading the Obligati-

on

(56)

on and History of his Death, he gets up unknown to you, and you are laid down in his Place, as afore said, according to the *English* Method ; and this is all the Difference between the *French* and *English* in their making of Masons.

Maſ. What was said to you then ?

Anſ. As I lay upon my Back, he gave me the whole Account how *Hiram* was found, and of his rising and taking the Three Ruffians that murder'd him.

Our Master *Hiram* being missing, as he did not come to view the Work as usual, so King *Solomon* made great Enquiry after him, and could not hear any Thing of him, therefore he suppos'd him dead : The Twelve Fellow-Crafts that had recanted, hearing the said Report, their Consciences pricking them, went and acquainted King *Solomon*, with white Aprons and Gloves, as Badges of their Innocency ; and King *Solomon* sent them in search of the Three Ruffians which had absconded : They divided into Four Parts, Three North, Three South, Three East, and Three West : One of those Parties travell'd down to the Sea of *Joppa*; one of them sat himself down to rest, by the Side of a Rock, he hearing a frightful Lamentation in a Clift of the Rock. Oh ! that I had had my Throat cut a-cross, and my Tongue torn out by the Root, and that buried in the Sands of the Sea at Low-water Mark, a Cable Length from Shore, where the Tide ebbs and flows in 24 Hours,
rather

(57)

rather than I had been concerned in the Death of our Master *Hiram*. Says the other; Oh! that I had had my Heart torn from under my naked Left-Breast, and given to the Vultures of the Air as a Prey, rather than I had been concerned in the Death of so good a Master. But Oh! says *Jubelum*, I struck him more hard than you both, for I killed him; Oh! that I had had my body severed in two, one Part carried to the South, and the other to the North; my Bowels burnt to Ashes in the South, and the Ashes scattered before the Four Winds of the Earth, rather than I had been concerned in the Death of our Master *Hiram*,

This Brother hearing this sorrowful Lamentation, hailed the other Two, and they went into the Clift of the Rock, and took them and bound them, and brought them before King *Solomon*, and they owned what had pass'd, and what they had done, and did not desire to live; therefore *Solomon* order'd their own Sentences to be laid upon them: Says he, they have sign'd their own Death, and let it be upon them as they have said.

Jubela was taken out, and his Throat cut across, &c. *Jubelo*'s Heart was torn from under his naked Left-breast, &c. *Jubelum*'s Body was severed in two, and one Part carry'd to the South, and the other to the North, &c.

After this King *Solomon* sent those 12 Crafts to raise their Master *Hiram*, in order that he might be interred in *Sanctum Sanctorum*. And *Solomon* told them, that if they could not find a Key-word in him or about him, it was lost;

I   for

for there were but Three in the World that knew it, and it can never be deliver'd without we Three are together; but now One is dead, therefore it is loft. But for the future, the firft occafion'd Sign and Word that is fpoke at his raifing, fhall be his ever after. So they went to raife him; and when they had clear'd the Rubbifh, they faw their Mafter lie dead, in a bruifed Condition; for he having already lain 15 Days, they lifted up both their Hands above their Heads in a great Surprize, and faid, O Lord my God, (which is the grand Sign of a Mafter-Mafon.)

Maf. How was he rais'd, Brother, when they had thus found him lying dead?

Anf. By the Five Points of Fellowfhip.

Maf. What are the Five Points of Fellow-fhip?

Anf. He was taken by the enter'd Apprentice's Gripe, but the Skin is fuppofed to flip off; he was then taken by the Craft's Gripe, and that flipped alfo; then he was taken by a more firm Gripe, that is, their Four Fingers Nails of their Right-hand ftuck into the Wrift of his Right-hand, (which is the Gripe of a Mafter) and pulling it with all your Might, with your Right-foot to his Right-foot, and his Right-knee to your Right-knee, and his Right-breaft to your Right-breaft, and your Left-hand fupporting his Back, and whifper in his Ear, and fay, MAHHABONE; that is, almoft rotten to the Bone, which is the Mafter's Word.

Maf.

(59)

Maf. Brother, it feems that you could not be raifed but by the Five Points of Fellow-fhip : Pray will you explain them.

Anf. 1*ft.* Hand in Hand is, that I always will put forth my Hand to ferve a Brother as far as lies in my Power.

2*d.* Foot to Foot is, that I never will be a-fraid to go a Foot out of my Way to ferve a Brothe

3*d.* Knee to Knee is, that when I kneel down to Prayers, I ought never to forget to pray for my Brother as well as myfelf.

4*tb.* Breaft to Breaft, is to fhow I will keep my Brother's Secrets as my own.

5*tb.* The Left-hand fupporting the Back, is that I always will be willing to fupport a Bro-ther as far as lies in my Power.

The MASTER's Reasons.

Maf. WHY was you depriv'd of all Metal ?

Anf. Becaufe at the Building of *Solomon's* Temple, there was neither Axe, Hammer, or the Sound of any Metal Tool, heard in the Building of that wonderful Fabrick.

Maf. Why fo, Brother ?

Anf. Becaufe it fhould not be polluted.

Maf. How is it poffible, Brother, that fuch a large Building fhould be carry'd on, without the Sound of fome Metal Tool ?

I 2   *Anf.*

(60)

Anf. It was prepar'd in the Foreſt of *Leba-non*, and brought down upon proper Car-riages, and ſet up with wooden Mauls made for that Purpoſe.

Maſ. Why was both your Shoes taken from off your Feet ?

Anf. Becauſe the Place whereon I ſtood, when I was made a Maſon, was holy Ground ; for the Lord ſaid unto *Moſes*, pull off thy Shoes, for the Place whereon thou ſtandeſt is holy Ground.

Maſ. What ſupports your Lodge ?
Anf. Three great Pillars.

Maſ. What are their Names ?
Anf. Wiſdom, Strength and Beauty.

Maſ. Who do they repreſent ?
Anf. Three Grand-Maſters ; *Solomon*, King of *Iſrael*, *Hiram*, King of *Tyre* ; and *Hiram Abiff*, which was the Widow's Son who was killed.

Maſ. Were all thoſe Three Grand Maſters concerned in the building of *Solomon*'s Temple ?
Anf. They were.

Maſ. What was their Buſineſs ?
Anf. *Solomon* for finding Proviſion, and Mo-ney to pay the Hirelings ; *Hiram*, King of *Tyre*, for finding Materials for the Work ; *Hiram Abiff*, for performing the Work.

[*Thus concludes the Maſter's Part, which is ſufficient for all Lodges ; but ſome will en-large upon the aforeſaid Parts, and run out of the Rules of Maſonry.*]

The

(61)

✖✖✖✖✖✖✖✖✖✖✖✖✖✖✖✖✖✖✖✖✖✖✖✖✖✖✖✖

The Charge given to the Officers of a Lodge.

AND firſt of the Maſter belonging to the Chair; which they call inſtalling a Maſter for the Chair.

N. B. He kneels down in the South, upon both Knees; and the late Maſter gives him the following Obligation, before he reſigns the Chair.

Anſ.   I *W*----- *V*-------.

Of my own free Will and Accord, and in the Preſence of Almighty God, and this right worſhipful Lodge, dedicated to St. *John*, do hereby, and hereon, moſt ſolemnly and ſincerely ſwear, that I will not deliver the Word and Gripe belonging to the Chair whilſt I am in the Chair, or any Time hereafter, except it be to a Maſter in the Chair, or Paſt Maſter, him or them whom I ſhall find to be ſuch after juſt Trial and due Examination.

I furthermore do ſwear I will act as Maſter of this Lodge, till next St. *John*'s Day, and I will fill the Chair every Lodge Night, if I am within the Length of my Cable-Tow.

I alſo further promiſe that I will not wrong this Lodge, but I will do all Things for the Good of Maſonry in general; nor will I reign arbitrarily, but I will be agreeable to the reſt of the Brethren. I alſo will keep good Orders in this Lodge, as far as lies in my Power, 'till next St. *Jhon*'s Day.

All

(62)

All this I fwear with a firm and fteady Refolution to perform the fame, without any Hefitation in me whatfoever, under no lefs than
the Four former Penalties, *viz.*

1ft. My Throat cut a-crofs, &c.

2d. My Tongue torn out, &c.

3d. Hy Heart torn from my Left-breaft, &c.

4th. My Body fever'd in two, &c.

So help me God, and keep me ftedfaft in this
my Obligation belonging to the Chair.

[He kiffes the Book.]

Then the late Mafter takes off his Jewel
and puts it upon him, and takes him by the
Mafter's Gripe, and raifes him off his Knees,
and whifpers in his Ear the Word, which is
Chibbilum, or, an excellent Mafon; then
he flips his Hand from the Mafter's Gripe to
his Elbow, and ftrikes his Nails in as you do
in the other Gripe at the Wrift. This is the
Word and Gripe belonging to the Chair.

N. B. The fenior and junior Warden, and
Secretary, receive the fame Obligation as he in
the Chair, only with this Difference, they have
neither Gripe nor Word. Therefore I have
no Occafion to infert it over again, as it is
the fame, and the fame Penalties.

The *MASTER*'s Clap.

IS by holding both Hands above your Head, and ſtriking upon your Apron, and both Feet going at the ſame Time ready to ſhake the Floor down: this they call the Grand Sign of a Maſter Maſon. They give two Reaſons for this Sign, *viz.* When they ſaw their Maſter *Hiram* lye dead, they lifted up their Hands in a Surprize, and ſaid, O Lord, my God! *Second.* When *Solomon* dedicated the Temple to the Lord, he ſtood up, and lifting up both his Hands, ſaid, O Lord my God, Great art Thou above all Gods, for in this Hour will I adore thy Name.

Thus I finiſh the whole Three Degrees of the moſt ancient Free-Maſonry, *with the Gripe and Word belonging to the Chair.*

How

(64)

※※※※※※※※※※※※ : ※※※※※※※※※

*How to go through an Examination, at
the Door of a* Free-Mason's *Lodge ;
and get Admittance, though ever such
a Stranger.*

WHEN you come to the Door of the
Lodge, where the Tyler ftands with a
drawn Sword, afk him if there is any Admittance ; he'll fay, I will go in and afk.
Then the Mafter, or fome other Man, will
come out to prove you. Firſt draw your
Right-hand edge-ways a-crofs your Throat ;
he will fay, what is that ? You fay the due
Guard of an enter'd Apprentice ; then he will
take you by the firſt Joint of your Right-hand,
and prefs upon it with his Right-thumb Nail,
and fay, what is this ?

Anf. The Gripe of an enter'd Apprentice.

Maf. Has it got a Name ?
Anf. It has.

Maf. Will you give it me ?
Anf. I'll Letter it with you, or half it.

Maf. Begin.
Anf. B O-
Maf. A Z.
Anf. B O A Z.

Maf. Will you be off or from ?
Anf. From.

Maf.

(65)

Maſ. From what ?

Anſ. From an enter'd Apprentice to a Fel-low-Craft.

N. B. Then he will put his Thumb from off the Apprentice's Gripe towards the Crafts, or between both.

Maſ. What's this ?

Anſ. The Paſs-Word of a Craft.

Maſ. Will you give it me ?

Anſ. SHIBBOLETH.

Maſ. Paſs SHIBBOLETH.

N. B. Then he puts his Thumb to the ſecond Joint, and ſays what's this ?

Anſ. The Gripe of a Fellow-Craft.

Maſ. Has it got a Name ?

Anſ. It has.

Maſ. Will you give it me ?

Anſ. I'll Letter it with you, or half it with you.

Maſ. I'll Letter it with you.

Anſ. Begin.

Maſ. No, you begin.

Anſ. J

Maſ. A

Anſ. C

Maſ. H

Anſ. I

Maſ. N.

Anſ. JACHIN is the Word you demanded.

Maſ. Will you be off or from ?

Anſ. From.

Maſ. From what ?

Anſ. From a Craft to a Maſter,

K   *Maſ.*

(66)

Maf. Give me the Fellow-Craft's Sign?

N. B. Put your Right-hand to your Left-breaft, your Thumb upright, and your Left-hand above your Head, forming a Square, then he takes you by the Mafter's Gripe.

Maf. What's this?
Anf. The Gripe of a Mafter Mafon.

Maf. Has it got a Name?
Anf. It has, and fomething elfe thereunto belonging.

Maf. What is that, Brother, as I may venture to call you fo now, I believe.
Anf. The Five Points of Fellowfhip.

Maf. Will you give me them, Brother?

N. B. Firft draw your Hand a-crofs your Belly, then lift both Hands up above your Head, and fay, O Lord my God, and then take him by the Mafter's Gripe, which is your Right-hand to his Right-hand, and put your Right-foot to his Right-foot, your Right-knee to his Right-knee, your Right-breaft to his Right-breaft, and your Left-hand to his Back, and whifper in his Ear, and fay, MAHHABONE.

This is the Five Points of Fellowfhip, and Word and Gripe thereunto belonging, as has been before defcrib'd. Thefe are all the Signs, Gripes and Words, that are ufed amongft Mafons at this Day.

All

(67)

All the Words explained that belongs to the GRIPES.

In *Hebrew* thus

The APPREN-TICE's Word is BOAZ.	בֹּעַז	It fignifies Strength, and it belongs to the Senior-Warden. You may have feen him carry it at Burials.
The CRAFT's Word is JACHIN.	צָכִין	This fignifies to eftablifh in the Lord, and it belongs to the Junior Warden. They are about twenty Inches long, to reprefent the two Pillars, Boaz and Jachin, as aforefaid.
The CRAFT's Pafs-Word is SHIBBOLETH.	שִׁבֹּלֵת	This fignifies Plenty, or an Ear of Corn and Fall of Water, which is Peace and Plenty. The Battle was fought in a Corn-Field, near a Fall of Water. This Word difcovers the Enemy. Vide the Twelfth Chapter of Judges.
The MASTER's Word is MAHHABONE.	מַחֲבֹן	This fignifies rotten, or decayed almoft to the Bone. It is the Word that is whifpered in your Ear at the raifing of your Mafter, and is never to be fpoke out; for they receive it as folemn as the Name of God.
The MASTER's Pafs-Word is TUBALCAIN.	תֻּבַלכַן	The Signification of this is, that he was the Inventor of Brafs, Iron, and other Metals : His Father was the Father of Mufick : He rofe from Cain, of the Fifth Generation; and his Son, Tubalcain, became excellent in all Metals, which Hiram improved. Vide the Fourth Chapter of Genefis. *NOTE.*

72

(68)

N O T E.

THE Mafter always fits in the Eaft, or ftands with the Bible before him ; and if it is the Apprentices Lecture, he opens it about the Second Epiftle of *Peter*, with the Compaffes laid thereon, and the Points of them covered with a little Box Square or *Lignum Vitæ*, about 4 Inches each Way, and the Points of the Compaffes points to the Weft, and the Two Points of the Square points to the Eaft. If it is the Craft's Lecture, the Mafter fhews one Point of the Compaffes, the Bible being open the 12th Chapter of *Judges*. If it is the Mafter's Lecture, the Bible is opened about the 7th Chap. of the Firft Book of *Kings*, and both the Points of the Compaffes is fhewn upon the Square. This is the Form they fit in when they work, as they call it.

The Reafon of their drinking Three Times Three is, becaufe there were antiently but Three Words, Three Signs and Three Gripes ; but there have been Three added, *viz.* The Grand Sign of a Mafter, the Pafs-Gripe of a Fellow-Craft, and Pafs-Word, which is Twelve in all for you to remember, *viz.* The Word, Sign and Gripe of an enter'd Apprentice is Three : The Word, Sign, Gripe, Pafs-Gripe and Pafs-Word of a Fellow-Craft is Five : and the Mafter hath Four, *viz.* The Sign, the Grand Sign, the Gripe and Word, which is Twelve, as aforefaid.

F I N I S.

(69)

A New and Correct List of all the *English*
Regular Lodges in *Europe*, *Afia*, *Africa*,
and *America*, according to their Seniority
and Conftitution.

By Order of the Grand Master.

Brought down to the Year 1768.

N. B. In the following LIST, M ftands for Monday, Tu for Tuefday, W for Wednefday, Th for
Thurfday, F for Friday, Sa for Saturday.

1 QUEEN's Arms, St. Paul's Church-Yard, 2d
W. Every 4th W there is a Mafter's Lodge.
It is alfo the Weft-India and American Lodge.

2 Horn, Weftminfter, 2d Th. Both the above conftituted Time immemorial.

3 Thatched Houfe, St. James's Street, Lodge of
Friendfhip, Jan. 17, 1721.

4 Crown and Rolls, Chancery-lane, 2d and 4th Tu.
Jan. 19, 1721.

5 Angel, St. Mary le Bonne, 1ft Th, Jan. 28, 1721.

6 Salmon and Ball, Charles-ftreet, Soho-fquare, 1ft
and 3d W, Feb. 27, 1722.

8 Running Horfe, David-Street, Grofvenor-fquare,
4th W, May, 1722-3.

9 Dundee-Arms, at their own Private-Room, Wapping, 2d and 4th Th, 1722.

10 Mitre, in Globe lane, Chatham, 1ft and 3d M,
March 28, 1723.

11 King's Arms, Wandfworth, 1ft Tu, March 30, 1723.

12 Three Crowns, Eaft Smithfield, 2d and 4th F,
April 1, 1723.

13 Feathers, Cheapfide, late the Mourning Bufh, 2d
and 4th Monday, 1723.

14 Crown and Rolls, Chancery-Lane, 2d and 4th
Th, Aug. 4, 1723,

15 Golden Anchor, at the Ballaft Key, in Eaft
Greenwich, 2d and 4th Tu, Sept. 11, 1723.

16 Globe, Fleet-Street. 1ft Th, Sept. 18, 1723.

17 Swan, Whitecrofs ftreet, Hatton-Garden, 4th
Th, Oft. 20, 1723,

L   18 Pewter

70   A LIST of REGULAR LODGES.

18 Pewter Platter, Crofs-ftreet, Hatton Garden,
2d and 4th Th, Dec. 24. 1723.

19 Thatched Houfe, Norwich, St. Lawrences Parifh,
1ft Th, 1724.

20 Dolphin, Chichefter, 3d W. July 17, 1724.

21 Three Tuns, Portfmouth, 1ft and 3d F, four
o'Clock, 1724,

22 George, Ironmonger Lane, 2d and 4th M, Jan.
22, 1724.

23 Queen's Head, at Stockton upon Tees, County
of Durham, 1ft and 3d F, Feb. 1724.

24 Sun, Ludgate-ftreet, 1ft and 3d M, April 1725.

25 Crofs Keys, Henrietta-Street, Covent-Garden,
1ft and 3d Tu, May 23. 1725.

26 St. Alban, St. Alban-Street, 3d M, Jan. 31, 1727.

27 Three Fleur de-Luce's, St. Barnard Street,
Madrid, 1ft Su, 1727.

28 Crown, little Cranbourn-Alley, Leicefter Fields,
1ft and 3d Th, 1728.

29 Swan, Elephant Stairs, Rotherhith, 2d Th, 1728.

30 Gibralter, at Gibralter, 1ft Tu, Nov. 1728.

31 Lion, Lynn Regis, Norfolk, 1ft F, Oct. 1, 1729.

32 ——————— Jan. 22, 1729.

33 ——————— Jan. 24, 1729.

34 Albermarle Arms, Dover Street, 2d and 4th Tu,
March 25, 1730.

35 ———————

36 Red Crofs, Barbican, 1ft W, 3d a Mafter'sLodge,
May 22, 1730.

37 White Lion, Putney, Th, neareft full Moon,
July 17, 1730.

38 ——————— Sept. 7, 1730.

39 King of Pruffia, Anchor Street, Bethnal-green,
1ft Friday, Jan. 26, 1730.

40 ———————

41 Old Magpye, Bifhopfgate-Street, 2d M, 1730.

42 Wind Mill, Rofemary Lane, 1ft M, 1730.

43 Angel, Macclesfield, Chefhire, 1731.

44 St. John of Jerufalem, Clerkenwell, 3d and 4th
W, Dec. 17, 1731.

45 ———————

46 Salutation and Cat, Newgate-Street, 1ft and 3d
M, Jan. 11, 1731.

47 King's Arms, St. Margaret'sHill, Southwark, 3d
M, Feb. 2, 1731.

48 Green

A LIST of REGULAR LODGES.   7**3**

48 King's Arms, Leigh in Lancashire, Feb. 22.

49 A la Ville de Tonerre, Rue des Boucheries a Paris, 1st M, April 3, 1732.

50 Turk's Head, Gerrard Street, Soho, 2d and 4th Tu, May 25, 1732.

51 King's Arms, Mary-le-bone Street, Picadilly, 2d and 4th Tu, Jan. 12, 1732.

52 Bacchus and Tun, at Hoxton, 3d, Th, June 12, 1732.

53 Lion and Cock, St. Michael's Alley, Cornhill, 3d Tu, Sept. 8, 1732.

54 Royal Oak, Darby, 1st and 3d Tu, Sept. 14, 1732.

55 Anchor and Hope Lodge, Bolton-le-more, Lancashire, Th. on or before Full Moon, Nov. 9. 1732.

56 Three Swans, Salisbury, 1st and 3d W, Dec. 27, 1732.

57 West-Cowes, Isle of Wight, 2d and 4th M, Feb. 17, 1732.

58 Swan, Chelsea, 2d and 4th Th, March 3, 1732.

59 White Bear, Bath, 1st and 3d Tu, May 18, 1733.

60 Mitre, Fleet-Street, 1st and 3d M, May 23, 1733.

61 Red Lion, Bury, Lancashire, next Th. to every Full Moon, July 26, 1733.

62 Talbot, Stourbich, Worcestershire, every W, Aug. 1, 1733.

63 Sun, St. Paul's Church Yard, 2d and 4th W, December 27, 1733.

64 King's Head, New Street, Birmingham, 1st and 3d F, 1733.

65 Royal Exchange, Boston, New-England, 2d and 4th Sa, 1733.

66 Valenciennes, French Flanders, 1733.

67 Oxford Inn, Plimouth Dock, 1st and 3d W, 1734.

68 Strong Man, East-Smithfield, late the Ship at the Hermitage, 1st and 3d Th, Feb. 17, 1734.

69 King's Head near the Watch-House, High Holbourn, 2d and 4th W, June 11, 1735.

70 Horn, Fleetstreet, Steward's Lodge, Publick Nights, 3d W in March and September.

71 In Holland, 1735.

72 Dorothy Jones's, in Swalewell, near Newcastle upon Tyne, 1st M, June 24, 1735.

73 Castle, at Aubigney in France, 1st M, Aug. 12, 1735.

L 2   74 Nov.

72   A LIST of REGULAR LODGES.

74 Nov. 12, 1735.

75 Savannah, at Savannah, in the Province of Georgia, 1735.

76 Angel, Colc. ester, 2d and 4th M, 1735.

77 Fountain, Gateshead, Newcastle upon Tyne, 2d and 4th W, March 8, 1735.

78 Green Man, Shrewsbury, 1st M, April 16, 1736.

79 Rising Sun, Fashion Street, Spittle Fields, 2d and 4th W, June 11, 1736.

80 King's Head, Norwich, last Thursday, 1736.

81 Th. Custom House by the Dock, Liverpool, 1st W, June 25, 1736.

82 Orange Tree, Bloomsbury-Square, 1st M, Aug. 16, 1736.

83 Swan, Wolverhampton, 1st and 3d Tu, Sept. 20, 1736.

84 Half Moon, Cheapside, 2d and 4th F, Dec. 2, 1736.

85 Star, ColemanStreet, 1st and 3d M, Dec. 21, 1736.

86 Caveac Tavern, Spread Eagle Court, Finch lane, Cornhill, 2d and 4th W, Dec. 31, 1736.

87 ————Jan. 24, 1736.

88 ————Feb 14. 1736.

89 Three Tuns, Spittlefields, 2d and 4th F, April 18, 1737.

90 Chapman's Coffee House, Sackville Street, 1st and 3d Tu, Aug. 24, 1737.

91 Talbot Inn, Strand, 1st Tu, Sept. 21, 1737.

92 Sun, Milk Street, Honey Lane-Market, 1st and 3d Tu, Dec. 8, 1737.

93 Angel, Shipton Mallet, Somersetshire, 1st and 3d M Dec. 12, 1737.

94 Parham Lodge, Parham, Antigua. Jan. 31, 1737.

95 Swan, Gloucester, 1st and 3d F, March 28, 1738.

96 Crown Tavern, Leadenhall Street, 2d Tu, May 3, 1738.

97 Rose and Crown, Halifax, in Yorkshire, 2d and 4th W, July 12, 1738.

98 The great Lodge at St. John's, Antigua, 2d and 4th W, Nov. 22, 1738.

99 Fox, near the Square, Manchester, 2d and 4th M, 1738.

100 Three Compasses, High-Holbourn, 2d and 4th M, Jan. 27, 1738.

101 Coach and Horses, Watergate Street, Chester, 2d Tu, Feb. 1, 1738.

103 Red

A LIST of REGULAR LODGES.   73

103 Red Lion, Hornchurch, in Effex, 1ft P, March 13, 1738.

104 Baker's Lodge, St. Mary's Street, St. John's Antigua. March 14, 1738.

105 The Mother Lodge, Kingfton, Jamaica, 1ft and 3d Sa, April 14, 1739.

106 April 24, 1739.

107 Scotch Arms, the Mother Lodge, at St. Chriftopher's, held at Baffeterre, 1ft Th, June 21, 1739.

108 Crown and Ball, Playhoufe-Yard, Black Friars, 1ft Tu, Aug. 24, 1739.

109 Eaft-India Arms, John Street, Blacks-Fields, Horfleydown, 1ft and 3d W, Oct. 8, 1739.

110 Albemarle Arms, South-Audley Street, 2d and 4th W, Oct. 25, 1739.

111 Queen's Head, Grays-Inn Gate, Holbourn, 3d M, Dec. 7, 1739.

112 King's Head, in the Poultry, 3d W, Jan. 1739.

113 Private Room, Laufanne, in the Canton of Bern in Switzerland, Feb. 2, 1739.

114 Three Lyons, Banbury, Oxfordfhire, every Full-Moon, if on Th, or the Th, before, March 31, 1740.

115 Ship, James Street, Covent-Garden, 2d Tu, June 26, 1740.

116 Fountain, High Street, Briftol, 1ft and 3d Tu, July 10, 1740.

117 The Third Lodge, at Calcutta, in the Eaft-Indies 1740.

118 St. Michael's Lodge, in Barbadoes, 1740.

119 Bunch of Grapes, Decker-ftreet, Hamburgh, every other Th, Oct. 23, 1740.

120 George, Whitehaven, Cumberland, 2d M, March 19, 1740.

121 Three Cranes, High-ftreet, Haverford Weft, South Wales, April 14, 1741.

122 Two Chairmen, Little Warwick Street, Chairing Crofs, 2d and 4th Th, in Winter, 2d Th, in Summer, April 13, 1742.

123 Old Road, at St. Chriftophers, Jan. 17, 1742.

124 Union, Franckfort in Germany, 2d and 4th Tu, Jan. 17, 1742.

125 Three Horfe Shoes, Leominfter, in the County of Hereford, Oct. 11, 1742.

126 Port Royal Lodge, Jamaica, 1742.

127

74   A LIST of Regular Lodges.

127 Angel, Dolgelly in Merionethshire, North-Wales, 1st Tu, Sept. 17, 1743.

128 St. George, Emperor's Court, Hamburgh, every other W,' Sept. 24, 1743.

129 ———

130 New Lodge at Copenhagen, Denmark, Oct 25. 1745.

131 St. Jago de la Vego, in Jamaica, April 29,1746.

132 Angel, Norwich, 2d and 4th Tu, May 9, 1747.

133 A new Lodge in St. Euftatia, Dutch Island, West-Indies, June 6, 1747.

134 Prince George's Head, Plimouth, 1st and 3d M, May 1, 1748.

135 June 15, 1748.

136 Queen's Head, Norwich, 3d Tu, Jan. 5, 1749.

137 Sun, at Cambridge, 2d M, March, 31, 1749.

138 Lodge of Orange, at Rotterdam, May 5, 1764.

139 St. Martin's Lodge, at Copenhagen, in Denmark, Oct. 9, 1749.

140 Sun, St. Peter's Mancroft, Norwich, 2d and 4th W, Jan. 9, 1749.

141 ———

142 ———

143 ———

144 St. Chriftopher's, at Sandy Point, July 20, 1750.

145 King and Miller, St. Bennet's Norwich, 2d and 4th W, Feb. 12, 1751.

146 King's Arms, Falmouth, 2d and 4th Th, May 20, 1751.

147 Angel, Great Yarmouth, in Norfolk, June 6, 1751.

148 King's Head, Weft-Street, Gravefend, 1st and 3d Th, June 8, 1751.

149 King's Head, Fenchurch-ftreet, the Sea Captain's Lodge, 3d Tu, Aug. 29, 1751.

150 ———

151 King's Arms, at Helfton in Cornwall, in Cornwall, 1st and 3d Tu, April 14, 1752.

152 St. John's Lodge, at Bridge Town, in the Ifland of Barbadoes, 4th M, April 23, 1752.

153 Ship, Leadenhall-ftreet, late the Bell at Aldgate, 2d and 4th M, July 13, 1752.

154 The George, the Corner of Maggot's Court, Piccadilly, 3d Tu, Aug. 21, 1753.

155

A LIST of REGULAR LODGES.   75

155 Mafon's Arms, at Truro, in Cornwall, 1ft and 3d Tu, Sept. 22, 1752.

157 At Chardenagore, the Chief French Settlement, in Bengal, Eaft-India.

157 At Madrafs, in Eaft-India.

158 At the Hague, in Holland.

159 St. Peter's Lodge, in the Ifland of Barbadoes, 1ft and 3d Sa. Dec. 15, 1752.

160 Jan. 7, 1753.

161 Lion and Goat, Grofvenor Street, 2d and 4th M, Feb. 24, 1753.

162 Crown and Horfefhoe, Corner of Bartlet's Buildings, Holbourn, 2d W, March 5, 1751.

163 White Hart, Shug Lane, Piccadilly, 1ft M.

164 Lilly Tavern, Guernfey, May 10, 1753.

165 Nag's Head, Wine Street, Briftol, 2d and 4th Tu, Auguft 22, 1753.

166 Vine, High Holbourn, 2d and 4th Tu, in Winter, and 4th Th, in Summer, Oct. 23, 1753.

167 Shakefpear, Market Street, Carmarthen, South Wales, 1ft and 3d M, Oct. 24, 1753.

168 King's Head, Prince's Street, Cavendifh Square, 2d and 4th W, Nov. 5. 1753.

169 Church Style, St. Peter's Mancroft, Norwich, 3d W, Nov. 10, 1753.

170 Evangelift's Lodge, at Antigua, Nov. 10, 1753.

171 At Amfterdam, Nov. 30, 1753.

172 Royal Oak at Prefcot, in Lancafhire, W next before Full Moon, Dec. 20, 1753.

173 The Royal Exchange Lodge, in the Borough of Norfolk, Virginia, 1ft Th, Dec. 22, 1753.

174 Jan. 31, 1754.

175 Crown, Holywell Lane, Shoreditch, 1ft M.

176 Private Room, at Redruth, in Cornwall, 1ft and 3d Th, Feb. 14, 1754.

177 Feb. 18, 1754.

178 Mitre, Union Street, Weftminfter, 2d Tu, March 2, 1754.

179 Three Tuns, North Cornsford, Norwich, 1ft and 3d Monday, March 4, 1754.

180 Swan, Ramfgate, in the Ifle of Thanet, 2d and 4th M, March 8, 1754.

181

76 A LIST of Regular Lodges.

181 Parrot, Cow-Lane, in Leeds, first Wednesday, March 28, 1754.

182 Three Tuns, Cambridge, 4th M, March 28, 1754.

183 The Angel and Porter, Golden Lane, Barbican, first Monday, April 5, 1754.

184 Marquis of Granby's Head, near St. George's Church, Southwark, 1st Wednesday, April 13, 1754.

185 ———— May 13, 1754.

186 Three Compasses and Punch Bowl, Silver-street, Golden Square, 2d and 4th Thursday, June 4, 1754.

187 Pelican, Leicester, first and third Tuesday, Aug. 21, 1754.

188 Bear, Cardiff, Glamorganshire, South Wales, second M, August 1754.

188 Bear, Cowbridge, Glamorganshire, last Monday, Sept. 1754.

190 No. 2. St. Eustatia, Dutch Island, West Indies, 1754

191 Queen's Head, Lowstoffe, in Suffolk, second Monday, October 29, 1754.

192 Chequers, Chairing Cross, second Tuesday, November 2, 1754.

193 Horn, Doctor's Commons, 2d and 4th Monday, December 14, 1754.

194 Crompton's Coffee house, Manchester, first and third Thursday, Feb. 4, 1755.

195 No. 8. the King's own Regiment of Foot, first and third Tuesday, February 15, 1755.

196 Turk's Head, King-street, Bloomsbury, second and fourth Friday in Winter, second Friday in Summer, March 2, 1755.

197 Jack of Newbury, Chiswell Street, first and 3d Wednesday, April 5, 1755.

198 Horseshoe, in Jermyn street, 2d and 4th Friday, May 5, 1755.

199 Star, Penzance, in Cornwall, 2d and 4th Wednesday, June, 14, 1755.

200 King's Arms, Tower Street, Seven Dials, first and third Monday, June 17, 1755.

201 The Duke, St. Bennet, Norwich, first and third Monday, June 17, 1755.

202 The Lodge of Charity at Amsterdam, June 24, 1755.

203

A LIST of Regular Lodges.

203 Eagle and Caftle, Chefter, every other Monday, June 24, 1755.

204 Lion, Beccles, in Suffolk, July 14, 1755.

205 Swan Tavern in York Town, Virginia, 1ft and third Wednefday, Auguft 1, 1755.

206 The Twins, Norwich, firft and third Friday, Sept. 16, 1755.

207 Nag's Head, Sunderland, Durham, firft Friday, Oct. 7, 1755.

208 The Grand Lodge Fredrick, at Hanover, Nov. 25, 1755.

209 Dog and Bull, Northgate-ftreet, Chefter, December 2, 1755.

210 Swan, Rider's Court, Cranborne-Alley, Leicefter Fields, firft and third Monday, Jan. 20, 1756.

211 A Lodge in Capt. Bell's Troop, in the Right Hon. Lord Ancram's Regiment of Dragoons, February 7, 1755.

212 Crown and Anchor, Strand, 2d and 4th Friday, Feb. 26, 1751.

213 A Lodge at Wilmington, on Cape Fear River, in the Province of North Carolina, March, 1755.

214 Merlin's Cave, Old Shambles, Liverpool, April, 15, 1755.

215 The Lodge of Peace at Amfterdam, September, 23, 1756.

216 ———— April 30, 1756.

217 White Horfe, Corner of New Burlington Street, firft and third Thurfday, December 2, 1756.

218 At the Marquis of Carnavon, at Sunderland, firft and third Tuefday, January 14, 1757.

219 In the Parifh of St. Mary, in the Ifland of Jamaica, Feb. 17, 1757.

220 Nag's Head, Vine Street, Briftol, fecond and fourth Thurfday, February 17, 1757.

221 At Parliament Coffee-Houfe, Parliament Street, fecond and fourth Wednefday, Feb. 14, 1757.

222 Star, at Lynn Regis, in Norfolk, 4th Wednefday, Feb. 21, 1757.

223 Dove and Branch, in the Parifh of St. Lawrence, Norwich, fecond Wednefday, March 23, 1757.

224 Sancta Croix, Danifh Ifland in the Weft-Indies, 1756.

225 Cock, the Head of the Side, Newcaftle upon Tyne, firft Monday, October 13, 1737.

M   226

A LIST of Regular Lodges.

226 Bacchus's Tun, Bloomsbury Market, second Monday, May 14, 1757.

227 Sun, at Shadwell, first and third Monday, Oct. 31, 1757.

228 The Lodge of Regularity, at Amsterdam, Nov. 21, 1757.

229 Long-Acre Coffee-house, first and third Friday, Dec. 20, 1757.

230 St. Michael's Lodge, in the City of Schwerin, in the Dutchy of Mecklenburg, May 15, 1754.

231 Cock, in the Parish of St. Mary, Norwich, every other Saturday, February 18, 1758.

232 Three Crowns, Southside Street, Plymouth, second and fourth Monday, March 1, 1758.

233 Duke of Beaufort, on the Quay, Bristol, second and fouth Tuesday, March 8, 1758.

234 Lodge at Bombay, in the East Indies, March 24, 1758.

235 Mercer's Arms, Mercer's Street, Long Acre, third Wednesday, August 6, 1758.

236 Swan at Yarmouth, Norfolk, the Sea Captain's Lodge, January 1, 1759.

237 Three Crowns at Plymouth, the second Division of Marines, January 2, 1759.

238 St. James's Lodge, at Barbadoes, May 20, 1758.

239 New Inn, at Exeter, second and last Friday, 1752.

240 Sun, at Newton Abbot, Devonshire, second Tuesday, March 17, 1759.

241 The Angel, in the West Town of Crediton, Devon, first Monday, April 21, 1759.

242 Royal Oak, Portsmouth Common, second and fourth Friday, April 21, 1759.

243 Compass and Square, Barnard Castle, Durham, first Monday, April 21, 1759.

244 Mermaid, at Windsor, third Monday, June 6, 1759.

245 Temple Lodge, at Bristol, first and third Monday, July 2, 1759.

246 Lebeck's Head in the Strand, third Friday Aug. 24, 1759

247 Prince George Lodge, in George Town Winyau, South Carolina, once a Month, 1743.

248 Union Lodge, Charles Town, South Carolina, second and fourth Thursday, May 3, 1755.

249

A LIST of Regular Lodges.

249 A Mafter's Lodge, Charles Town, South Carolina, fecond and fourth Thurfday, March 22, 1756.

250 Port Royal, at Beaufort, Port Royal Carolina, every other Wednefday, September 15, 1756.

251 ———

252 Black Bull, at Mighton's Gate, Hull, fecond and laft Thurfday, Auguft 20, 1759.

253 King's Head, Canterbúry, 1ft and 3d Wednefday, Jan. 14, 1763.

254 A Lodge on board the Vanguard, January 16, 1760.

255 St. Andrew's Crofs, the Marines Lodge, near the Hermitage, firft and third Friday.

256 Three Crowns, at Guernfey, firft and third Monday.

257 Guy Earl of Warwick, Gray's-Inn-Lane, firft Friday, Nov. 27, 1760.

258 Golden Lyon, near the Bridge, Leeds, Yorkfhire, fecond Wednefday and Fourth, a Mafter's Lodge, January 8. 1761.

259 Punch Bowl, Stone Gate, York, 1ft and 3d Monday, Jan. 12, 1761.

260 Feathers, Cheapfide, the Caledonian Lodge, firft and third Thurfday, March 9, 1761.

261 Square and Compafs, Whitehaven, Cumberland, fecond Monday, May 4, 1761.

262 Lord Granby's Head, Dover, 1ft and 3d Thurfday, May 8, 1761.

263 Sun, at Darlington, Yorkfhire, laft Saturday, June 19, 1761.

264 Spread Eagle, Wifbich, firft and third Tuefday, Aug. 8, 1761.

265 ———, Aug. 20, 1761.

266 Union Lodge, Crow Lane, Barbadoes, firft Wednefday, September 17, 1761.

267 A Lodge at Kingfton upon Hull, fecond and fourth Thurfday, Oct. 27, 1761.

268 All Saints Lodge, at Wooler, Northumberland, January 1, 1762.

269 St. George's Lodge, at the Half Moon, Exeter, fecond and fourth Friday, January 20, 1762.

270 Green Man, Ipfwich, Suffolk, January 21, 1762.

271 Royal Fredrick, at Rotterdam, Jan. 25, 1726.

272 No. 2, St. John's Lodge, New York, fecond and fourth Wednefday, December 27, 1757.

A LIST of Regular Lodges.

273. George, Birmingham, 1ſt. and 3d. Tu, Feb. 23, 1762.

274. A Private Room, at Appledore, Devon, March, 18, 1762.

275. Eighth lodge at Calcutta, in the Eaſt Indies, Feb. 7, 1761.

276. Hole in the Wall, at Colne, Lancaſhire.

277. The Merchants Lodge, at Quebec, Mar. 2, 1762.

278. ——, May 8, 1762.

279. Somerſet-houſe Lodge, at the King's Arms, New Bond-ſtreet, May 22, 1762.

280. Globe, High-ſtreet, Salop, 1ſt. and 3d. Wedneſday, May 28, 1762.

281 Fleece, at Barnſtable, Devon. 1ſt. and 3d. Monday, May 28, 1762.

282 Eaſt India Arms, at Deal, June 8, 1762.

283 Duke's Head, Lynn Regis, Norfolk, third Friday, June 9, 1762.

284 La Loge des Freres Réunis, at Amſterdani, June 16, 1762.

285 Lodge of Inhabitants of Gibraltar, July 12, 1762.

286 St. David's Lodge, King's Head and Maſon's Arms, Holywell, North Wales, ſecond and fourth Wedneſday, January 13, 1761.

287 Half moon, at Otley, in Yorkſhire, firſt Monday, Auguſt 16, 1762.

288 Virtutis & Artis Amici, at Amſterdam, September 16. 1762.

289 At Workington, in Cumberland, firſt Monday, September 22, 1762.

290 Green Dragon, at Hereford, firſt Thurſday, October 12, 1756.

291 King's Arms, Portſmouth, 1ſt and 3d Monday, November 2, 1762.

292 Feathers, Market Place, Nottingham, 3d Tueſday, Jan. 31, 1763.

293 The Sun, Univerſity Lodge, Cambridge, ſecond Thurſday March 1, 1763.

294 Crown, Rocheſter, 2d and 4th Friday, Mar. 17, 1763

295 Black Bull, at Hexam, Northumberland, firſt and third Wedneſday, March 8, 1763.

296 Stag, at Chippenham, Perfeƈt Union Lodge, 1ſt Monday, Maſter's Lodge, third Tueſday, May 1763.

297 Lodge at Richmond, Yorkſhire, ſecond Monday, May 4, 1763.

298

A LIST of Regular Lodges.

298 Bear, at Havant, in Hampſhire, 1ſt and 3d Wedneſday, 1763.

299 St. Mark's Lodge, South Carolina, Feb. 8, 1763.

300 The Lodge of Regularity, at St. John's Hall, Black River, Muſquito Shore, firſt and third Tueſday, March 8, 1763

301 City of London, at Dover, firſt and third Wedneſday, Auguſt 2, 1763.

302 Lodge in a private Room, at Stubbington, Hants, Aug. 10, 1763.

303 Seven Stars, in the pariſh of St. Thomas the Apoſtle, near Exeter, 1ſt and 3d Wed. Aug. 10, 1763.

304 Marquiſs of Granby's Head, Durham, firſt Tueſday, September 8. 1763.

305 Lodge at the Hall at Burnley, Lancaſhire, every Saturday neareſt the Full Moon, Octorber 9, 1763.

306 The Union Lodge, at the Coopers Arms, in Camomile-ſtreet, Biſhopſgate-ſtreet, firſt and third Saturday, November 7, 1763.

307 Royal Mecklenburgh Lodge, at the Hermione, and Active Frigate, Compton-ſtreet, St. Ann's, fourth Friday, November 28, 1763.

308 Sarracen's Head, Chelmsford, Eſſex, ſecond and fourth Monday, January 18, 1764.

309 Lodge of Amity, at the Haul Over, up the River Beliſe, in the Bay of Honduras, firſt and third Tueſday, September 21, 1763.

310 Faulcon, Eaſt-ſtreet, Graveſend, ſecond and fourth Thurſday, March 4, 1764.

311 Royal Edwin Lodge, at Lyme Regis, in Dorſetſhire, firſt and third Monday, April 6, 1764.

312 The Door to Virtue, at Hildeſheim in Germany, Dec. 27, 1762.

313 Royal Lodge, Thatched Houſe, St. James's-ſtreet, late the New Lodge, at the Horn, Weſtminſter, firſt Wedneſday, April 4, 1764.

314 Vitruvian Lodge, Swan and Faulcon, Roſs, Herefordſhire, May 3, 1764.

315 St. George's Lodge, at Taunton, Somerſetſhire, July 13, 1764.

316 Swan, at Kendal, Weſtmorland, firſt Wedneſday, July 31, 1764.

317 Three Crowns, at Harwich, ſecond and fourth Thurſday, Auguſt 9, 1764.

318 Nag's Head, at Lymington, Hants, firſt and third Friday, Auguſt 16, 1764.

319

A LIST of Regular Lodges.

319 White Hart, at Melton, in Kent, every other Wednesday, August 28, 1764.

320 Salutation, at Topsham, Devon, second and fourth Wednesday, August 30, 1764.

321 Globe, St. Saviour's Church-yard, Southwark, second Tuesday, October 23, 1764.

322 Club Inn, Isle of Ely, first Wednesday, October 23, 1764.

323 Fountain, at Helsey, Hants, first and third Monday, Nov. 7, 1764.

324 Pon's Coffee-house, Castle-street, Leicester-fields, second and fourth Monday.

325 Half Moon, Cheapside, Caledonian Lodge, first Monday, November 15, 1764.

326 Swan, at Bridgwater, Somerset, first and third Monday, December 4, 1764.

327 Rose and Crown, Mill-street, Dock Head, South-wark, first and third Tuesday, December 11, 1764.

328 Rose, at Sittingbourn, in Kent, first and third Tuesday.

329 Crown, at Swaffham, Norfolk, first Monday, December 17, 1764.

330 King of Sweden, Wapping Dock, first and third Tuesday, January 8, 1765.

331 Fountain, Ludgate Hill, French Lodge, second and fourth Thursday, January 20, 1765.

332 Boar's Head Lodge, at the Fountain, Snow-hill, first and third Wednesday, January 29, 1765.

333 Goose and Gridiron, St. Paul's Church-yard, first and third Thursday, January 29, 1765.

334 Dolphin and Horseshoe, Lamb's-conduit-passage, Red-lion-street, third Friday, January 22, 1765.

335 George, Wardour-street, Soho, Operative Masons, first and third Tuesday, March 13, 1765.

336 George, Shug-lane, fourth Monday, March 22, 1765.

337 Bell, Brecon, South Wales, first and third Monday.

338 Lion and Lamb, Pool, Dorset, 1st and 3d Wednesday, April 1, 1765.

339 White Hart, Strand, April 16, 1765.

340 Rose and Crown, Sheffield, Yorkshire, second Friday, April 19, 1765.

341 At Alost, in Flanders, June 5, 1765.

342 Rose and Crown, Coventry, first and third Monday, June 20, 1765.

343

A LIST of Regular Lodges.

343 Queen's Head, Chelfea, fecond Friday in Summer, fecond and fourth in Winter, June 29, 1765.

344 White Lion, Rye, in Suffex, firft and third Tuefday, July 10, 1765.

345 Flafk, at Chelfea, third Tuefday, July 17, 1765.

346 Lodge at Joppa, in Baltimore County, Maryland, Auguft 8, 1765.

347 La Sageffe St. Andrew, at the Grenades, May 1, 1764.

348 Greyhound and Shakefpear Inn, and Tavern, at Bath.

349 A Lodge, No. 1. conftituted in the Town of St. Hilary, in the Ifland of Jerfey.

350 New Inn, Melkfham, Wilts, firft and third Wednefday, December 7, 1765.

351 At Tortola and Beef Ifland, firft and third Wednefday, December 7, 1765.

352 Fleece, at Warrington, in Lancafhire, laft Monday, November 8, 1765.

353 Lodge, No. 1. at Madrafs.

354 Lodge, No. 2. at Madrafs.

355 Lodge, No. 3. at Madrafs.

356 Lodge, No. 1. at Bencoolen.

357 Blue Boar, at Norwich.

358 Red Lion, (the Royal Edwin,) at Fakenham, in Norfolk, fecond Monday, and laft Monday a Mafter's Lodge, December 30, 1765.

359 Lodge of Perfeverance, at Amfterdam, 2d and 4th Saturday.

360 Ship, at St. Ive's, Cornwall, firft and third Tuefday, July 16, 1765.

361 George and Crown, at Wakefield, Yorkfhire, Feb. 15, 1766.

362 King's Arms Punch-houfe, Shad Thames, firft Monday, February 22, 1766.

363 Englifh Lodge, at Bourdeaux, met fince the Year 1732, March 8, 1766.

364 Mitre, (Operative Mafons,) Union-ftreet, Weftminfter, 2d and 4th Wednefday, May 17, 1766.

365 Dolphin, at Shoreham, firft and third Thurfday, April 18, 1766.

366 Black Lion, at Greenwich, 2d and 4th Tuefday, May 26. 1766.

367 White Hart Inn, Lewes, in Suffex, firft and third Wednefday, May 29, 1766.

368 Swan, Oxford-road, 3d Wed. June 23, 1766.

369

A LIST of REGULAR LODGES.

369 Recruiting Serjeant, Carlisle, Cumberland, first and third Friday, August 1, 1766.

370 Globe, at Exeter, August 6, 1766.

371 Weavers Arms, Dorset-street, Spitalfields, fourth Tuesday, July 26, 1766.

372 Union Lodge, Princes-street, opposite Merchants Hall, Bristol, 2d and 4th Wednesday, Sep. 9. 1766.

373 King's Head Tavern and Coffee-house, Islington, second Friday, September 10, 1766.

374 Black Horse, Oxenden-street, Haymarket, September 16, 1766.

375 Le Loge de Sagesse, a Havre, Normandie, en France, October 8, 1766.

376 Crown and Anchor Lodge, (constituted the Lodge of Immortality,) in the Strand, 1st and 3d Tu. 1766.

377 White Hart, Exeter, October 31, 1766.

378 St. Nicholas Lodge, (private Room,) Newcastle upon Tyne, November 29, 1766.

379 Sion Lodge, (private Room,) North Shields, Northumberland, November 29, 1766.

380 Thistle and Crown, near Tower-hill, second and fourth Monday, December 4, 1766.

381 Star, Water-gate-street, Chester, third Thursday, November 28, 1766.

382 Rose and Crown, (Lodge of Peace,) opposite the Custom-house, Thames-street, second and fourth Thursday, December 19, 1766.

383 King's Arms, Bennet-street, Southwark, (the Black Friars Bridge, Lodge,) second and fourth Tuesday, February 9 1767.

384 Castle, Holborn, February 16, 1767.

385 Upper Swan, Market-street-lane, Manchester, 1767

386 Sun, at Chatham, February 17, 1767.

387 White Hart, Folkstone in Kent, first and third Thursday, March 16, 1767.

388 Lodge at Grenoble, in France, March 18, 1767.

389 Admiral Hawke, Jerusalem Lodge, on the Quay, at Bristol, April 1, 1767.

390 The Constitution, Bedford-street, Covent garden, first and third Friday, April 11, 1767.

391 Bull's Head, Little Windmill-street.

F I N I S.

Jachin and Boaz

JACHIN AND BOAZ;
OR, AN
AUTHENTIC KEY
TO THE DOOR OF
FREE-MASONRY,
Both ANCIENT and MODERN.

Calculated not only for the Inftruction of every New made MASON, but alfo for the Information of all who intend to become Brethren.

CONTAINING,

I. A circumftantial Account of all the Proceedings in making a Mafon, with the feveral Obligations of an ENTERED APPRENTICE, FELLOW-CRAFT, and MASTER; the Prayers, and alfo the Sign, Grip, and Pafs-Word of each Degree, with the Ceremony of the Mop and Pall.

II. The Manner of opening a Lodge, and fetting the Craft to work.

III. The *Entered Apprentice, Fellow-Craft*, and *Mafter's Lectures*, verbatim, as delivered in all Lodges; with the Song at the Conclufion of each Part.

IV. The Origin of Mafonry; Defcription of *Solomon's* Temple; Hiftory of the Murder of the Grand Mafter *Hiram* by the three Fellow-Crafts; their Difcovery and Punifhment; the Burial of *Hiram* by King *Solomon's* Order, with the Five Points of Fellowfhip, &c.

V. The Ceremony of the Inftalment of the Mafters of different Lodges on St. *John's* Day.—Defcription of the Regalia, &c.

VI. Ceremonies ufed at the Funeral of a Mafon.

VII. A fafe and eafy Method propofed by which a Man may obtain Admittance into any Lodge, without paffing through the Form required, and tnereby fave a Guinea or two in his Pocket.

VIII. Anthems, Odes, Songs, &c.

Illuftrated with

A Beautiful FRONTISPIECE of the REGALIA, JEWELS, and Emblematical ORNAMENTS belonging to MASONRY.

AND

An Accurate Plan of the Drawing on the Floor of a Lodge,

Interfperfed with Variety of

NOTES and REMARKS,

Neceffary to explain and render the whole clear to the meaneft Capacity,

To which is now added,

A New and accurate LIST of all the Englifh Regular Lodges in the World, according to their Seniority, with the Dates of each Conftitution, and Days of Meeting.

By a GENTLEMAN belonging to the Jerufalem Lodge; a frequent Vifitor at the Queen's Arms, St. Paul's Church-yard; the Horn, in Fleet-ftreet; Crown and Anchor, Strand; and the Salutation, Newgate-ftreet.

Try me; prove me.

A NEW EDITION, greatly Enlarged and Improved.

LONDON:

Printed for E. NEWBERY, the Corner of St. Paul's Church-yard; VERNOR and HOOD, Poultry; and CHAMPANTE and WHITROW, Jewry-ftreet, Aldgate.

1797.

PREFACE TO THE FIRST EDITION.

TO ALL

FREE-MASONS.

THE Author of the following Pages has the Honour of being well refpected in moft of the Lodges of Reputation in this Metropolis, and has been a frequent Vifitor at the Queen's Arms, St. Paul's Church-yard; the Globe, in Fleet-ftreet; the Jerufalem, at Clerkenwell; Half-moon, Cheapfide; Crown and Anchor in the Strand; Salutation, Grey-Friars; and feveral others of lefs Note.

An Earneft Defire of becoming a perfect Mafter of MASONRY, and the Succefs he met with in his firft Attempt, has rendered him capable of revealing thofe Myfteries to the World, which, till now, have been kept fecret as the Grave.

He acquired his Knowledge at firft from fome loofe Papers belonging to a Merchant to whom he was nearly related, who had been a Member of the Queen's Arms, St. Paul's Church-yard. This Relation dying about ten Years ago, the Editor became poffeffed of his Effects; and on looking over his Papers, among others he found fome Memorandums or Remarks on MASONRY, which excited his Curiofity fo far, that he refolved on accomplifhing his Scheme, without going through the Ceremonies required by the Society.

The Remarks of his Friend abovementioned furnifhed Hints fufficient to make a Trial on an intimate Acquaintance, a FREE MASON, who readily gave him the Sign in the Manner he expected. After a more narrow Infpection on the Part of his Friend, fuch as, where he was made, and when, &c. &c. (to all which he anfwered with great Readinefs) he received an Invitation to fpend an Evening at a Tavern in the Strand, with feveral Acquaintances.

A 2

Elated

Elated by this Succefs, he boldly advanced with his Company; all of whom belonged to the Lodge, and were well known by the TYLER at the Door. After the ufual Ceremony, in which he gave full Satisfaction, he was admitted and took his Seat. That Night he faw two MAKINGS*, and came off full of Spirits.

Soon after he went to another Lodge, where he diftinguifhed himfelf greatly in anfwering the Queftions propofed by the Mafter, which he acquired from his Friend's Manufcripts of the EN-TERED APPRENTICE, and FELLOW-CRAFT's Lectures.

His Regard to the Society, and Refpect to the Public is the only inducement to this Publication, which is intended not only to affift thofe who have been lately made, and ftill remain ignorant of the true Foundation of the Art, but alfo to give all that have an Inclination to become Mafons an Opportunity of confidering the Advantages and Difadvantages of the Engagements and Oaths by which they are bound.—Such is the Intention of this Undertaking; and the Editor flatters himfelf the Brotherhood will not condemn his Officioufnefs in this Refpect, as it will rather ftrengthen than hurt the Intereft of the Society; the Fear of going through the Ceremony, which hitherto has been reprefented in fuch frightful Shapes, being the greateft Obftacle to its future Welfare and Increafe.

The Editor's Ambition is to pleafe; and the Work is fubmitted to the only proper Judges, viz. his Brethren the FREE MASONS; to whom he begs leave to declare, that no private or public Quarrel, the View of Gain, nor any other Motive than the Public Good could ever have induced him to write upon this fubject; and he declares to the World, that the following is the whole of true MASONRY in all its Branches.

---

* *Makings*, the Term ufed in the circular Letters to the Members of the Lodge, acquainting them that New Members are to be admitted the next Lodge Night.

ADVER-

ADVERTISEMENT.

SINCE the former Edition of this Pamphlet was put to Press, the Author has received from his Publisher several anonymous Letters, containing the lowest Abuse and scurrilous Invectives; nay, some have proceeded so far as to threaten his Person. He requests the Favour of all enraged Brethren, who shall chuse to display their Talents for the future, that they will be so kind as to pay the Postage of their Letters, for there can be no Reason why he should put up with their ill Treatment, and pay the Piper into the Bargain. Surely there must be something in this Book very extraordinary; a Something they cannot digest, thus to excite the Wrath and Ire of those hot-brained Mason-bit Gentry! But however unwilling the Editor may be to publish *all* the Letters and Messages he has received on this occasion, yet he cannot be so deficient in returning the Compliment, as to conceal one, which notwithstanding the Threatenings contained in it, appears to be wrote with very little meaning, and he has (sans ceremonie) ventured to publish it verbatim.

For R. S. at Mr. Wm. Nicholls at the Paper Mill St. Paul Church Yard London.

" R S.   London.
" Try thee prove thee* I shall find thee a Scandalous Stinking powcatt, thou pretends to have declared the truth of Masonry to the World. And has Imposed a Lie on the Public Not in one part But in all Parts thon Mentions, I shall meet the in a few Days and will give thee Satisfaction Such a Pike thonk Scandalous Villain Deserves."

The Original of this spirited Letter, with the Post-mark to authenticate it, is left in the hands of Mr. Nicoll, Bookseller, in St. Paul's Church-yard, who has the Editor's leave to shew it to any Gentleman desirous to peruse so pretty an Epistle; and strict Orders are given the Publisher to receive none, for the future, that are not Post-paid.

. Those Gentlemen who so often send for JACHIN and BOAZ, and desire the Publisher to tie it up and seal it carefully, to hide it from the Messenger, may safely continue their Commissions, and the Publisher will carefully observe their Order.   R. S.

* Alluding to the Motto in the Title Page, taken from the Fellow Craft's Lecture.

DESCRIPTION *of the* REGALIA *and* EMBLEMATICAL FIGURES *used in* MASONRY, *represented in the* FRONTISPIECE.

1. THE two Pillars called JACHIN and BOAZ, the first signifying *strength*, the second *to establish in the Lord*.
2. The Holy Bible opened, as an Emblem that it should be the Rule of our Faith.
3. The Compass and Square, to square our Actions, and keep them within Bounds, the Master's Emblem or Jewel, which is suspended with a Ribbon round the Neck, and always worn when the Lodge is opened, and on public Days of Meeting, Funerals, &c.
4. The Level, the Senior Warden's Emblem or Jewel.
5. The 24 Inch Gauge, to measure Mason's Work.
6. The Key, the Treasurer's Emblem.

7. The

7. The Sword, presented to the naked left Breast of the Apprentice.
8. The Cable, or Rope, put round the Neck of every new-
made Mason at the Time of Making.
9. The Trowel, an Instrument of great Use among Masons.
10. The Gavel, or setting Maul, used in building Solomon's
Temple, the first Grand Work of Masonry.
11. The Plumb, Level, Compass, and Plumb Rule, the Junior
Warden's Emblem.
12. The small Hammer, to knock off superfluous Pieces.
13. The Cross Pens, the Secretary's Emblem.
14. A Coffin, with a Figure of the maimed body of Hiram (the first
Grand Master) painted on it. He was murdered by three
Fellow-Crafts, for refusing to reveal the Secret. See p. 31.
15. The Hand Plummet, for taking Perpendiculars.
16. The Sun rising in the East, emblematical of the Master-Mason, standing in the East, and setting the Men to Work.
17. The Seven Stars, an Astronomical Emblem, frequently en-
graved on the Medals worn by Masons.
18. The Moon, that rules the Night. See p. 14.
19. The Candlesticks, placed in a triangular form.
20. The Columns, used by the Senior and Junior Wardens in
the Lodge. See p. 37.
21. Two black Rods, carried by the Senior and Junior Deacons.
22. The Three Steps and Pavement.
23. Entrance or Porch to Solomon's Temple.
24. The Terrestrial and Celestial Globes, representing the Works
of Creation.
25. A Machine used by Masons for forming Triangles.
26. The large Rule for measuring the Work.
27. The three Step Ladder used in Masonry.
28. Hiram's Tent.
29. The White Aprons and Gloves, Emblems of Innocence.
30. Eye of Providence, the Great Superintendent of all the
Works of the Universe, and Masonry represented as under
its immediate Influence.

The Frontispiece is a Medallion, in Imitation of those Medals,
or Plates that are common among the Brotherhood. These Medals
are usually of Silver, and some of them highly finished and ornamented, so as to be worth ten or twenty Guineas. They are suspended round the Neck with Ribbons of various Colours, and
worn on their Public Days of Meeting, at Funeral Processions,
&c. in Honour of the Craft. On the Reverse of these Medals it
is usual to put the Owner's Coat of Arms, or Cypher, or any other
Device that the Owner fancies, and some even add to the Emblems other Fancy Things that bear some Analogy to Masonry.

The Candlesticks, &c. in many Lodges are curiously wrought,
the Chair in which the Grand Master sits, as well as those of the
Masters of inferior Lodges, are richly carved with Emblematical Figures; their Aprons are bound with Ribbons of various
Colours; and, in short, every Thing belonging to them is finished in the most elegant Taste.

a   AN

AN

AUTHENTIC KEY

TO THE DOOR OF

FREE-MASONRY.

T HE Origin * of the Society called Free-Masons is
said by some to have been a certain Number of Per-
sons who formed a Resolution to rebuild the Temple
of *Solomon* †. This appears from the Lecture, or
rather History, of the Order, at the Making or Rais-
ing of a Member to the Degree of Master, which is fully described in the following Work. But I am inclined to think,

---

*. The Rise of this Science (says an original Record) was before the
Flood. In the 4th Chapter of Genesis it is said, There was a Man named
Lamech who had two Wives named *Adah* and *Zillah*; by *Adah* he begat
two Sons, *Jabal* and *Jubal*; by *Zillah* he begat one Son, called *Tubal
Cain*, and a Daughter named *Naamah*. These children found out the
Beginning of all the Crafts in the World; *Jabal* found out Geometry;
he divided Flocks of Sheep, and built the first House of Timber and Stone.
Jubal found out the Art of Music, and was the Father of all those who
handled the Harp. *Tubal Cain* was the Instructor of all Artificers in Iron
and Brass; and his Daughter discovered the Craft of Weaving.
  † By an old Record it appears, that King *Solomon* confirmed all the Charges
which King *David* had given to Masons in *Jerusalem*; and that the Temple was
finished, A. M. 3000. In the Year 43, after *Christ*, Masons first came into
England, and built the Monastery of *Glastonbury* in *Somersetshire*.

that

that the chief Defign of the Eftablifhment is to rectify the
Heart, inform the Mind, and promote the Moral and Social
Virtues of Humanity, Decency, and good Order, as much as
poffible in the World : and fome of the Emblems of Free-
Mafons confirm this Opinion, fuch as the Compafs, Rule,
Square, &c.

In all Countries where Mafonry is practifed, or eftablifhed
at this time, there is a Grand Mafter ; but formerly there
was only one Grand Mafter, and he was an *Englifhman.*
HIS ROYAL HIGHNESS GEORGE PRINCE OF WALES
is the Perfon on whom the Dignity is now beftowed,
who governs all the Lodges in *Great Britain*, and has
the power of delivering the Conftitutions and Laws of the
Society to the Mafters who prefide over the fubordinate
Affemblies : which Conftitutions muft always be figned by
the Grand Secretary of the Order.——The Grand Mafter
can hold a Meeting or Lodge when he thinks proper, which
is generally the fecond *Saturday* in every Month in the
Summer, but oftener in the Winter.

The other Lodges meet regularly twice a Month in the
Winter Half-Year, and once a Month in the Summer ; and
the Members of each Lodge pay Quarterly, from 3s. 6d. to
5s. into the Hands of the Treafurer ; and this generally de-
frays the Expence of their Meetings.

There are alfo Quarterly Communications or Meetings,
held, at which are prefent the Mafter and Wardens of every
Regular Conftitution in and near *London*, where the feveral
Lodges fend, by the faid Wardens, different Sums of Money
to be paid into the Hands of the Treafurer General, and ap-
propriated to fuch charitable Ufes as the Grand Mafter, and
the Mafters of the different Lodges under him, think proper ;
but thefe Charities are chiefly confined to Mafons only. Such
as have good Recommendations as to their Behaviour and Character, will be affifted with Five, Ten, or Twenty Pounds ;
and lefs Sums are diftributed to the indigent Brethren, in Proportion to their Wants, and the Number of Years they have
been Members. At thefe Quarterly Communications, large
Sums are likewife fent from Lodges in the moft remote Parts
of the World, viz. in the *Eaft* and *Weft Indies*, and Accounts
tranfmitted of the growth of Mafonry there. The State of
the Funds of the Society are likewife communicated to the
Company, and the Deliberations of the Meeting taken down
by the Secretary, who lays them before the Grand Mafter at
the yearly Meeting.

The Number of Members which compofe a Lodge is in-
determinate ; but it is no Lodge except there are prefent
one Mafter, three Fellow-Crafts, and two Apprentices.

When

(3)

When a Lodge is met, there are two principal Officers under the Master, called Senior and Junior Wardens, whose Business it is to see the Laws of the Society strictly adhered to, and the Word of Command given by the Grand Master regularly followed.

It must be remarked, that the Authority of a Master, though Chief of the Lodge, reaches no farther than he is himself an Observer of the Laws; should he infringe them, the Brethren never fail to censure him; and if this has no Effect, they have a Power of deposing him, on appealing to the Grand Master, and giving their Reasons for it; but they seldom proceed to this Extremity.

As no Doubt the Reader chuses to be made acquainted with every Circumstance of the Ceremony of making a Mason, I shall begin with the following Directions, and proceed regularly in the Description of what further concerns Masonry.

A Man desirous of becoming a Free Mason, should endeavour to get acquainted with a Member of some good Lodge, who will propose him as a Candidate for Admission the next Lodge-Night. The Brother who proposes a New Member, is likewise obliged to inform the Brethren of the Qualifications of the Candidate *. Upon this it is debated whether or not he shall be admitted; and it being arried in the Affirmative, the next Step is to go with the proposer the ensuing Lodge-Night.

The Evening being come when a Lodge is to be held, which generally begins about Seven in the Winter, and Nine in the Summer, as previous Notices are sent to the Members for this Purpose; the Masons are punctual to Time, and it frequently happens, that, in half an Hour, the whole Lodge, to the Number of Fifty or Sixty, are assembled.

The Master, the two Assistants, Secretary, and Treasurer, begin with putting over their Necks a blue Ribbon of a triangular Shape; to the Master's Ribbon hangs a Rule and Compass, which is in some Lodges made of Gold, though in others only gilt: the Assistants, Senior Wardens, and the other Officers, carry the Compass alone.

The Candles are placed upon the Table in the Form of a Triangle; and in the best Lodges the Candlesticks are finely carved with emblematical Figures. Every Brother has an Apron made of white Skin, and the Strings are also of Skin; though some of them chuse to ornament them with Ribbons

---

* For the Good of this, and all other Societies, it were to be wished a more strict Regard was paid, on the Part of the Proposers, to the Character and Morals of every Candidate.

B

cf

(4)

of various Colours. On the Grand Days, such as Quarterly
Communications, or General Meetings, the Grand Officers
Aprons are finely decorated, and they carry the Rule and
Compass, the Emblems of the Order.

When they sit down to the Table, the Master's Place is
on the East Side, the Bible being opened before him, with
the Compass laid thereon, and the Points of them covered
with a Lignum Vitæ or Box Square; and the Senior and
Junior Wardens opposite to him on the West and South. On
the Table is likewise Wine, Punch, &c. to regale the Brethren, who take their Places according to their Seniority.
Being thus seated, after a few Minutes, the Master proceeds
to * *Open the Lodge* in the following Manner:

Manner of Opening a Lodge, and setting the Men to Work.

Master, to the Junior Deacon. What is the chief Care of a
Mason?

Ans. To see that the Lodge is tyled.

Mas. Pray do your duty.

[The Junior Deacon gives Three Knocks at the Door; and
the † Tyler on the other Side of the Door answereth, by
giving Three Knocks. Then the Junior Deacon tells the
Master, saying]

Ans. Worshipful, the Lodge is tyled.

Master, to the Junior Deacon. Pray where is the Junior
Deacon's Place in the Lodge?

Deacon's Ans. At the Back of the Senior Warden; or at
his Right-Hand, if he permits him.

Mas. Your Business there?

Ans. To carry Messages from the Senior to the Junior
Warden, so that they may be dispersed round the Lodge.

Master, to the Senior Deacon. Pray where is the Senior
Deacon's Place in the Lodge?

Senior Deacon's Ans. At the Back of the Master; or at
his Right-Hand if he permits.

Mas. Your Business there?

Ans. To carry Messages from the Master to the Senior
Warden.

Mas. The Junior Warden's Place in the Lodge?

Deacon's Ans. In the South.

---

* To open a Lodge, in Masonry, signifies that it is allowed to speak freely
among one another of the Mysteries of the Order.

† A Tyler is properly no more than a Guard, or Centinel placed at the
Lodge Door, to give the Sign when any one craves Admittance, that the
Wardens may come out and examine him; but he is always one of the
Brethren.

2   *Master.*

(5)

Master, to the Junior Warden. Why in the South?

Junior Warden's Anf. The better to obferve the Sun at high Meridian, to call the Men off from Work to Refrefhment, and to fee that they come on in due Time, that the Mafter may have Pleafure and Profit thereby.

Maf. Where is the Senior Warden's Place in the Lodge?

Junior Warden's Anf. In the Weft.

Master, to the Senior Warden. Your Bufinefs there, Brother?

Senior Warden's Anfwer. As the Sun fets in the Weft to clofe the Day, fo the Senior Warden ftands in the Weft to clofe the Lodge, to pay the Men their Wages, and difmifs them from their Labour.

Maf. The Mafter's Place in the Lodge?

Senior Warden's Anf. In the Eaft.

Maf. His Bufinefs there?

Senior Warden's Anf. As the Sun rifeth in the Eaft to open the Day, fo the Mafter ftands in the Eaft to open his Lodge, and fet the Men to work.

[Then the Mafter takes off his Hat, and declares the Lodge open as follows]

Mafter. "This Lodge is open, in the Name of Holy "St. *John,* forbidding all Curfing, Swearing, or Whifper- "ing, and all prophane Difcourfe whatever, under no lefs "Penalty than what the Majority fhall think proper."

The Mafter gives three Knocks upon the Table with a wooden Hammer, and puts on his Hat, the Brethren being uncovered : He then afks, if the Gentleman propofed laft Lodge-Night is ready to be made? and on being anfwered in the Affirmative, he orders the Wardens to go out and prepare the Perfon, who is generally waiting in a Room at fome Diftance from the Lodge Room by himfelf, being left there by his Friend who propofed him. He is conducted into another Room, which is totally dark ; and then afked, Whether he is confcious of having the Vocation neceffary to be received? On anfwering Yes, he is afked his Name, Surname, and Profeffion. When he has anfwered thefe Queftions, whatever he has about him made of Metal is taken away, as Buckles, Buttons, Rings, &c. and even the Money in his Pocket*. Then they uncover his Right Knee, and put his Left Foot with his Shoe on into a Slipper+; hoodwink him with a Handkerchief, and leave him to his Re-

---

* In fome Lodges they are fo particular, that the Candidate's Clothes are taken off, if there be Lace on them.

+ This is not practifed in every Lodge ; fome only flipping the Heel of the Shoe down.

flection

(6)

flection for about Half an Hour. The Chamber is also
guarded within and without by some of the Brethren who
have drawn Swords in their Hands. The Person who pro-
posed the Candidate stays in the Room with him; but they
are not permitted to converse together.

During this Silence, and while the Candidate is preparing,
the Brethren in the Lodge are putting every Thing in order
for his Reception there; such as drawing the annexed Figure
on the Floor at the upper Part of the Room; which is generally done with Chalk and Charcoal intermixed; though
some Lodges use Tape and little Nails to form it; which
prevents any Mark or Stain on the Floor. It is drawn East
and West. The Master stands in the East, with the Square
hanging at his Breast, the Holy Bible opened at the Gospel
of St. *John*, and three lighted Tapers are placed in the Form
of a Triangle in the Midst of the Drawing on the Floor.

The Proposer then goes and knocks three Times at the
Door of the Grand Apartment, in which the Ceremony is to
be performed. The Master answers within by three Strokes
with the Hammer, and the Junior Warden asks, Who comes
there? The Candidate answers (after another who prompts
him) " One who begs to receive Part of the Benefit of this
" Right Worshipful Lodge, dedicated to St. *John*, as many
" Brothers and Fellows have done before me." The Doors
are then opened, and the Senior and Junior Wardens, or
their Assistants, receive him, one on the Right, and the other
on the Left, and conduct him blindfolded Three Times *
round the Drawing on the Floor, and bring him up to the
Foot of it, with his Face to the Master †, the Brethren
ranging themselves on each Side, and making a confused
Noise, by striking on the Attributes of the Order, which
they carry in their Hands ‡.

---

* In some Lodges the Candidates are led Nine Times round; but as this
is very tiresome to the Person who is to undergo the Operation, his Patience being pretty well tired by being blinded so long beforehand, it is very
justly omitted.

† Many Lodges throw a fine Powder, or Rosin on the Floor, which with
the Illumination of the Room, has a pretty Effect.

‡ This Custom is not observed in all Lodges.

PLAN

PLAN *of the* DRAWING *on the* FLOOR *at the*
making of a MASON.

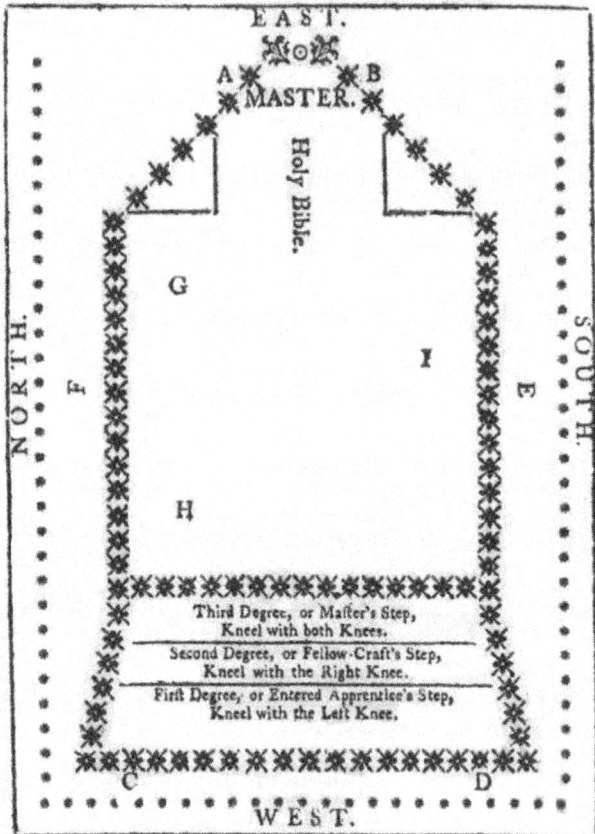

EAST.

A ✳ ✳ B
✳ MASTER. ✳

Holy Bible.

G

I

NORTH.

SOUTH.

F

E

H

Third Degree, or Master's Step,
Kneel with both Knees.
Second Degree, or Fellow-Craft's Step,
Kneel with the Right Knee.
First Degree, or Entered Apprentice's Step,
Kneel with the Left Knee.

C   D

WEST.

EXPLANATION.

A Senior Deacon, with a black Rod.
B Past-Master, with the Sun and Compasses, and a String of Cords.
C Senior Warden, with the Level, and a Column in his Hand.
D Junior Deacon, with a black Rod.
E Junior Warden, with a Column in his Hand.
F The Secretary, with Cross Pens.
G H I Candles.
✳ Masons standing round at the Ceremony.

When

(8)

When this Part of the Ceremony is ended, the Master who stands at the upper End, facing the Foot or Steps of the Drawing on the Floor, behind a low Arm-chair, asks the following Question, Whether you have a desire to become a Mason? and if it is of your own free Will and Choice? Upon which the Candidate answers, Yes. " Let him see " the Light," says the Master : They then take the Hand-kerchief from his Eyes, and whilst they are so doing, the Brethren form a Circle round him, with their Swords drawn in their Hands, the Points of which are presented to his Breast. The Ornaments borne by the Officers, the glit-tering of the Swords, and fantastic Appearance of the Bre-thren in White Aprons, creates great Surprise, especially to a Person, who for above an Hour has been fatigued with the Bandage over his Eyes ; and his Uncertainty concerning what is further to be done for his Reception, must, no Doubt, throw his Mind into great Perplexity *,

The Candidate is then directed to advance Three Times to a Stool at the Foot of the Arm-chair ; he is taught to step in a proper Manner by one of the Assistants. Upon the Stool are placed the Rule and Compass ; and one of the Brethren says to the Candidate to this Effect : " You are " now entering into a respectable Society, which is more " serious and important than you imagine. It admits of " nothing contrary to Law, Religion, or Morality ; nor " does it allow any Thing inconsistent with the Allegiance " due to His Majesty ; the Worshipful Grand Master will " inform you the rest †."

As soon as the Speaker has ended his Speech, he is de-sired to put his Right Knee upon the Stool, which is bare, as mentioned above ‡, and his left foot is put into a Slipper, with the Shoe on, or the Shoe slipped at the Heel, to repre-sent a Slipper.

The Candidate being in this Posture, the Worshipful Grand Master addresses him to the following Effect : " Do " you promise never to tell, write, or disclose, in any man-" ner whatever, the Secrets of Free Masonry and Free Ma-

---

* The ancient Masons made use of a Prayer inserted in the Apprentice's Lecture ; but the Moderns leave it out when they make a Brother.

† It is here to be understood, that in different Lodges this Speech varies : as also do the Forms of Making in some Respects, which may be seen in the Entered Apprentice's Lecture ; where the only proper and ancient Method is clearly pointed out.

‡ The ancient Custom was thus : The Candidate, though kneeling on his Right Knee, should have his Left Foot in the Air ; but this Position being fatiguing, it is omitted in most Lodges.

" sons,

(9)

" fons, except to a Brother at the Lodge, and in the Pre-
" fence of the Worſhipful Grand Maſter?" On which the
Perſon ſays, " I do." His Waiſtcoat is then unbottoned *,
and the Point of a Pair of Compaſſes † placed upon his
naked Left Breaſt, and he himſelf holds it with his Left
Hand, his Right Hand being laid upon the Goſpel opened at
St. *John*; when the following Oath is adminiſtered to him,
he repeating it after the Maſter :

THE OATH.

" I——A. B. of my own Free Will and Accord, and in
" the Preſence of Almighty God ‡, and this Right Wor-
" ſhipful Lodge, dedicated to St. *John*, do hereby, and herein
" moſt ſolemnly and ſincerely ſwear, that I will always
" hale, conceal; and never reveal any of the Secrets or
" Myſteries of Free Maſonry, that ſhall be delivered to me
" now, or at any Time hereafter, except it be to a true and
" lawful Brother, or in a juſt and lawful Lodge of Brothers
" and Fellows, him or them whom I ſhall find to be ſuch,
" after juſt Trial and due Examination. I furthermore do
" ſwear that I will not write it, print it, cut it, paint it,
" ſtint it, mark it, ſtain or engrave it, or cauſe it ſo to be
" done, upon any thing moveable or immoveable under the
" Canopy of Heaven, whereby it may become legible or
" intelligible, or the leaſt Appearance of the Character of a
" Letter, whereby the ſecret Art may be unlawfully obtained:
" All this I ſwear, with a ſtrong and ſteady Reſolution to
" perform the ſame, without any Heſitation, mental Reſer-
" vation, or Self-evaſion of Mind in me whatſoever; under
" no leſs penalty than to have my Throat cut acroſs, my
" Tongue torn out by the Root, and that it be buried in
" the Sands of the Sea, at Low Water Mark, a Cable's
" Length from the Shore, where the Tide ebbs and flows
" twice in twenty-four Hours. So help me God, and
" keep me ſtedfaſt in this my Entered Apprentice's Obliga-
" tion." [*He kiſſes the Book.*]

The new made Member is then taught the Sign, Grip,
and Paſs-word of the Entered Apprentice, which will be

* This is done leſt a Woman ſhould offer hẏ ſelf. If we believe the
Iriſh, there is ꜱ dẏ at this Time in *Ireland*, who has gone through the
whole Ceremony, and is as good a Maſon as any of them.

† The Ancients uſed a Sword or Spear inſtead of a Compaſs:

‡ The Form of the Oath differs in many Lodges, though this is the
ſtricteſt in Uſe; and in ſome Societies inſtead of ſaying, " In the Preſence
" of Almighty God," it runs thus, " I promiſe before the Great Architect
" of the Univerſe," &c.

ſeen

feen more clearly in the following Lecture belonging to that Part of Mafonry.

He is alfo learnt the Step, or how to advance to the Mafter upon the Drawing on the Floor, which in fome Lodges refembles the Grand Building, termed a Mofaic Palace, and is defcribed with the utmoft Exactnefs. They alfo draw other Figures, one of which is called the Laced Tuft, and the other, the Throne befet with Stars. There is alfo reprefented a perpendicular Line in the Form of a Mafon's Inftrument, commonly called the Plumb-Line; and another Figure which reprefents the Tomb of *Hiram*, the firft Grand Mafter, who has been dead almoft Three Thoufand Years. Thefe are all explained to him in the moft accurate Manner; and the Ornaments or Emblems of the Order are defcribed with great Facility. The Ceremony being now ended, the new-made Member is obliged to take a Mop out of a Pail of Water brought for that Purpofe, and rub out the Drawing on the Floor, if it is done with Chalk and Charcoal. Then he is conducted back, and every Thing that he was divefted of is reftored, and he takes his Seat on the Right Hand of the Mafter. He alfo receives an Apron, which he puts on; and the Lift of the Lodges is likewife given him.

The Brethren now congratulate the new-made Member; and all return to the Table to regale themfelves; when the Mafter propofes a Health to the young Brother, which is drank with the greateft Applaufe by the whole Body, the new Mafon fitting all the while. After which he, inftructed by a Brother, takes a Bumper, and drinks " To the Wor-" " fhipful Grand Mafter, the Senior and Junior Wardens, " the reft of the Officers and Members of the Lodge, wifh-" ing them Succefs in all their public and private Under-" takings, to Mafonry in general, and that Lodge in par-" ticular, craving their Affiftance." To which they anfwer, " they will affift him." And after he has drank, he throws his Glafs from him, and brings it back three Times, and then fets it down on the Table, the reft doing the fame in exact Order. This they call Firing; Then they clap their Hands Nine Times divided into Three, and ftop between each, keeping true Time.

The Reader having been led thus far, it is high Time to introduce the Apprentice's Lecture, which is intended not only to amufe, but likewife to inftruct him in the Part he is entered into. The readinefs of many of the Brethren in anfwering the Queftions, adds a Luftre to the Order, the Members vying with each other who fhall moft contribute to the Edification of their new Brother.

The

(11)

The Entered Apprentice's Lecture*.

Maf. BROTHER, is there any Thing between you and
me ?   *Anf.* There is, Right Worshipful.
Maf. What is it Brother, pray?   *Anf.* A Secret.
Maf. What is that Secret, Brother?   *Anf.* Masonry.
Maf. Then I presume you are a Mason ?
Anf. I am so taken and accepted amongst Brothers and
Fellows.
Maf. Pray what sort of a Man ought a Mason to be?
Anf. A Man that is born of a Free Woman.
Maf. Where was you first prepared to be made a Mason ?
Anf. In my Heart.
Maf. Where was you next prepared?
Anf. In a Room adjoining to the Lodge.
Maf. How was you prepared, Brother?
Anf. I was neither naked, nor clothed, bare-foot, nor
shod; deprived of all Metal; hood-winked, with a Cable
Tow about my Neck, where I was led to the Door of the
Lodge, in a halting moving Posture, by the Hand of a
Friend, whom I afterwards found to be a Brother.
Maf. How do you know it to be a Door, you being
blinded?
Anf. By finding a Stoppage, and afterwards an Entrance,
or Admittance.
Maf. How got you Admittance ?
Anf. By three Knocks.
Maf. What was said to you within ?
Anf. Who comes there?
Maf. Your Answer, Brother?
Anf. One who begs to have and receive Part of the Bene-
fit of this Right Worshipful Lodge, dedicated to St. *John*,
as many Brothers and Fellows have done before me.
Maf. How do you expect to obtain it ?
Anf. By being free born, and well reported.
Maf. What was said to you then ?   *Anf.* Enter.
Maf. How did you enter, and upon what ?
Anf. Upon the Point of a Sword or Spear, or some warlike
Instrument presented to my naked left Breast.
Maf. What was said to you then ?
Anf. I was asked if I felt any thing.
Maf. What was your Answer?

* The Reader is desired to observe, that here I give the *Whole* of the Lecture, as delivered in the primitive Time; but the modern Masons leave
out at least one-half.

    C   *Anf.* I did,

Anf. I did, but I could fee nothing.

Maf. You have told me how you was received; pray who received you? *Anf.* The Junior Warden.

Maf. How did he difpofe of you?

Anf. He delivered me to the Mafter, who ordered me to kneel down and receive the Benefit of a Prayer.

Brethren, let us Pray.

O LORD God, thou g at and univerfal Mafon of the World, and firft Buil of Man, as it were a Temple; be with us, O Lord, as thou haft promifed, when two or three are gathered together in thy Name, thou wilt be in the midft of them: Be with us, O Lord, and blefs all our Undertakings, and grant that this our Friend may become a faithful Brother. Let Grace and Peace be multiplied unto him, through the Knowledge of our Lord Jefus Chrift; And grant, O Lord, as he putteth forth his Hand to thy Holy Word, that he may alfo put forth his Hand to ferve a Brother, but not to hurt himfelf or his Family; that whereby may be given to us great and precious Promifes, that by this we may be Partakers of thy Divine Nature, having efcaped the Corruption that is in the World through Luft.

O Lord God, add to our Faith Virtue, and to Virtue Knowledge, and to Knowledge Temperance, and to Temperance Prudence, and to Prudence Patience, and to Patience Godlinefs, and to Godlinefs Brotherly Love, and to Brotherly Love Charity; and grant, O Lord, that Mafonry may be bleffed throughout the World, and thy Peace be upon us, O Lord, and grant that we may be all united as one, through our Lord Jefus Chrift, who liveth and reigneth for ever and ever. *Amen.*

Maf. After this Prayer, what was faid to you?

Anf. I was afked who I put my Truft in?

Maf. Your Anfwer, Brother? *An* In God.

Maf. What was the next Thing faid o you?

Anf. I was taken by the Right Hand, and a Brother faid, Rife up, and follow your Leader, and fear no Danger.

Maf. After all this, how was you difpofed of?

Anf. I was led three Times round the Lodge.

Maf. Where did you meet with the firft Oppofition?

Anf. At the Back of the Junior Warden in the South, where I gave the fame Three Knocks as at the Door?

Maf. What Anfwer did he give you?

Anf. He faid, Who comes there?

4   *Maf.*

(13)

Maſ. Your Anſwer?

Anſ. The ſame as at the Door, One who begs to have and receive, &c.

Maſ. Where did you meet with the ſecond Oppoſition?

Anſ. At the Back of the Senior Warden in the Weſt, where I made the ſame Repetition as at the Door. He ſaid, Who comes here? One who begs to have and receive, &c.

Maſ Where did you meet with the third Oppoſition?

Anſ. At the Back of the Maſter in the Eaſt, where I made the Repetition as before.

Maſ. What did the Maſter do with you?

Anſ. He ordered me back to the Senior Warden in the Weſt to receive Inſtructions.

Maſ. What where the Inſtructions he gave you.

Anſ. He taught me to take one Step upon the firſt Step of a right Angle oblong Square, with my left Knee bare bent, my Body upright, my right Foot forming a Square, my naked Right Hand upon the Holy Bible, with the Square and Compaſs thereon; my left Hand ſupporting the ſame; where I took that ſolemn Obligation or Oath of a Maſon.

Maſ. Brother, can you repeat that Obligation?

Anſ. I will do my Endeavour, with your Aſſiſtance, Wor-ſhipful.

Maſ. Stand up and begin.

[Here the Oath is repeated, as mentioned before. After repeating this Obligation, they drink a Toaſt to the Heart that conceals, and to the Tongue that never reveals. The Maſter in the Chair gives it, and they all ſay Ditto, and draw the Glaſſes acroſs their Throats, as aforeſaid.]

Maſ. Now, Brother, after you received the Obligation, what was ſaid to you?

Anſ. I was aſked what I moſt deſired.

Maſ. What was your Anſwer?

Anſ. To be brought to Light.

Maſ. Who brought you to Light.

Anſ. The Maſter and the reſt of the Brethren.

Maſ. When you was thus brought to Light, what were the firſt Things you ſaw?

Anſ. The Bible, Square, and Compaſs.

Maſ. What was it they told you they ſignified?

Anſ. Three great Lights in Maſonry.

Maſ. Explain them, Brother?

Anſ. The Bible to rule and govern our Faith; the Square to ſquare our Actions; the Compaſs to keep us within Bounds with all Men, particularly with a Brother.

C 2 *Maſ.*

(14)

Maf. What where the next Things that were shewn to you?

Anf. Three Candles, which I was told were three lesser Lights in Masonry.

Maf. What do they represent?

Anf. The Sun, Moon, and Master-Mason.

Maf. Why so, Brother?

Anf. There is the Sun to rule the Day, the Moon to rule the Night, and the Master-Mason his Lodge, or at least ought so to do.

Maf. What was then done to you?

Anf. The Master took me by the Right-Hand, and gave me the Grip and Word of an Entered Apprentice, and said, Rise, my Brother JACHIN,

> [Sometimes they shew you the Sign before the Grip and Word is given, which is JACHIN: It is the Entered Apprentice's Word, and the Grip thereto belonging is to pinch with your Right Thumb Nail upon the first Joint of your Brother's Right Hand.]

Maf. Have you got this Grip and Word, Brother?

Anf. I have, Right Worshipful.

Maf. Give it to your Brother.

> [Then he takes his next Brother by the Right Hand, and gives him the Grip and Word, as before described.]

The 1*ft* Brother gives him the Grip.

The 2*d* Brother says, What's this?

1*ft Bro.* The Grip of an Entered Apprentice.

2*d Bro.* Has it got a Name?   1*ft Bro.* It has,

2*d Bro.* Will you give it me?

1*ft Bro.* I'll letter it with you, or halve it.

2*d Bro.* I'll halve it with you.

1*ft Bro.* Begin.

2*d Bro.* No. You begin first.

1*ft Bro.* JA.

2*d Bro.* CHIN.

1*ft Bro.* JACHIN,

2*d Bro.* It is right, Worshipful Master.

Maf. What was the next Thing that was shewn to you?

Anf. The Guard or Sign of an Entered Apprentice*.

Maf. Have you got the Guard or Sign of an Entered Apprentice?

> [He draws his Right Hand across his Throat (as aforesaid) to shew the Master that he has.]

---

* The Guard or Sign as they call it, is by drawing your Right Hand across your Throat edgeways; which is to remind you of the Penalty of your Obligation, that you would sooner have your Throat cut across than discover the Secrets of Masonry.

Maf.

Maf. After this, what was faid to you?

Anf. I was ordered to be taken back, and invefted with what I had been divefted of; and to be brought again to return Thanks, and to receive the Benefit of a Lecture, if Time would permit.

Maf. After what you had been divefted of was reftored, what was next done to you?

Anf. I was brought to the North Weft Corner of the Lodge, in order to return Thanks.

Maf. How did you return Thanks?

Anf. I ftood in the North Weft Corner of the Lodge, and, with the Inftruction of a Brother, I faid, Mafter, Senior and Junior Wardens, Senior and Junior Deacons, and the reft of the brethren of this Lodge, I return you Thanks for the honour you have done me in making me a Mafon, and admitting me a member of this Worthy Society.

Maf. What was then faid to you?

Anf. The Mafter called me up to the North Eaft Corner of the Lodge at his Right Hand.

Maf. Did he prefent you with any thing?

Anf. He prefented me with an Apron, which he put on me: He told me it was a badge of Innocence, more ancient than the Golden Fleece or the *Roman* Eagle; more honoured than the Star and Garter, or any other Order under the Sun, that could be conferred upon me at that Time, or any Time hereafter.

Maf. What were the next Things that were fhewn you?

Anf. I was fet down by the Mafter's Right Hand, who fhewed me the Working Tools of an Entered Apprentice.

Maf. What were they?

Anf. The 24 Inch Gauge, the Square, and common Gavel or Setting Maul.

Maf. What are their Ufes?

Anf. The Square to fquare my Work, the 24 Inch Gauge to meafure my Work, the common Gavel to knock off all fuperfluous Matter, whereby the Square may fit eafy and juft.

Maf. Brother, as we are not all working Mafons, we apply them to our Morals, which we call fpiritualizing: Explain them.

Anf. The 24 Inch Gauge reprefents the 24 Hours of the Day.

Maf. How do you fpend them, Brother?

Anf. Six Hours to work in, fix Hours to ferve God, and fix to ferve a Friend or a Brother, as far as lies in my Power, without being detrimental to myfelf or family.

I come now to the Entered Apprentice's Reafons; but as the ceremony of drinking Healths among the Mafons takes up much of their Time, we muft ftop a little, in order to introduce

(16)

troduce some of them. The first is, " To the Heart that
" conceals, and the Tongue that never reveals ;" Then
" The King and Royal Family ;" and, " To all Brethren
" wheresoever dispersed *." The Pleasures they enjoy,
Purity of their Sentiments, and the uniformity that always
reign in their Assemblies, is far from being tiresom' or in-
sipid. I next proceed to the

Entered Apprentice's Reasons †.

Maf. WHY was you neither naked nor clothed, bare-
footed nor shod, with a Cable-Tow (or Halter)
about your Neck?

Anf. If I had recanted, and ran out in the Street, the People would have said I was mad ; but if a Brother had seen
me, he would have brought me back, and seen me done Jus-
tice by.

Maf. Why was you hood-winked ?

Anf. That my heart may conceal before my eyes did discover.

Maf. The second Reason, Brother ?

Anf. As I was in Darkness at that Time, I should keep
all the world in Darkness.

Maf. Why was you deprived of all Metal ?

Anf. That I should bring nothing offensive or defensive
in the Lodge.

Maf. Give me the second Reason, Brother ?

Anf. As I was poor and pennyless when I was made a Mason, it informed me that I should assist all poor and pennyless
Brethren as far as lay in my Power.

Maf. Brother, you told me you gave three distinct Knocks
at the Door : Pray what do they signify ?

Anf. A certain Text in Scripture.

Maf. What is that Text ?

Anf. " Ask, and you shall have ; Seek, and you shall find ;
" Knock and it shall be opened unto you."

Maf. How do you apply this Text in Masonry ?

Anf. I sought in my Mind ; I asked of my Friend ; I
knocked and the Door of Masonry became open unto me.

Maf. Why had you a Sword, Spear, or some other warlike Instrument presented to your naked Left Breast particularly ?

Anf. Because the Left Breast is the nearest the Heart, that
it might be the more a Prick to my Conscience, as it pricked
my Flesh at that Time.

* These Toasts or Healths are all drank with Three Times Three, which
is performed in a most regular Manner, and an Huzza at the End of each, as
before described.
† This in fact is only a Continuation of the Lecture.

Master.

(17)

Maf. Why was you led three Times round the Lodge?

Anf. That all the Brethren might fee I was duly prepared.

Maf. When you was made an Apprentice, why was your Left Knee bare bent?

Anf. Becaufe the Left Knee is the weakeft part of my body, and an Entered Apprentice is the weakeft Part of Mafonry, into which Degree I was then entering.

[Here the Brethren refume their Glaffes, and drink a Health fometimes to the Grand Mafter; at other Times to the Wardens, or other Officers, and then proceed.]

The form af a Lodge.

Maf. BROTHER, pray what makes a Lodge?

Anf. Right Worfhipful, a certain Number of Mafons met together to work.

Maf. Pray what Number makes a Lodge?

Anf. Three, Five, Seven, or Eleven.

Maf. Why do Three make a Lodge?

Anf. Becaufe there were Three Grand Mafons in the building of the world, and alfo that noble Piece of Architecture, Man; which are fo complete in Proportion, that the Ancients began their Architecture by the fame Rules.

Maf. The fecond Reafon, Brother?

Anf. There were three Grand Mafons at the building of Solomon's Temple.

Maf. Why do Five make a Lodge?

Anf. Becaufe every Man is endowed with Five Senfes.

Maf. What are the Five Senfes?

Anf. Hearing, Seeing, Smelling, Tafting, and Feeling.

Maf. What Ufe are thofe Five Senfes to you in Mafonry?

Anf. Three are of great Ufe to me, *viz.* Hearing, Seeing, and Feeling.

Maf. What Ufe are they Brother?

Anf. Hearing is to hear the Word; Seeing is to fee the Sign; Feeling is to feel the Grip, that I may know a Brother as well in the Dark as in the Light.

Maf. Why fhould feven make a Lodge?

Anf. Becaufe there are feven liberal fciences.

Maf. Will you name them, Brother?

Anf. Grammar, Rhetoric, Logic, Arithmetic, Geometry, Mufic, and Aftronomy.

Maf. Brother, what do thefe Sciences teach you?

Anf. Grammar teaches me the Art of Writing and Speaking the Language taught me according to the firft, fecond, and third Concord.

Maf. What doth Rhetoric teach you?

Anf. The Art of Speaking upon any Topic whatfoever.

Maf.

(18)

Maf. What doth Logic teach you?

Anf. The Art of Reafoning well, whereby you may find out Truth from Falfehood.

Maf. What doth Arithmetic teach you?

Anf. The Ufe of Numbers.

Maf. What doth Geometry teach you?

Anf. The Art of Meafuring, whereby the *Egyptians* found out their own Land, or the fame quantity which they had before the overflowing of the River *Nile*, that frequently ufed to water their Country, at which time they fled to the Mountains till it went c again, and this made them have continual Quarrels about their Lands.

Maf. What doth Mufic teach you, Brother?

Anf. The Virtue of Sounds.

Maf. What doth Aftronomy teach you?

Anf. The Knowledge of the Heavenly Bodies.

Maf. Why fhould Eleven make a Lodge, Brother?

Anf. There were Eleven *Patriarchs* when *Jofeph* was fold into *Egypt*, and fuppofed to be loft.

Maf. The fecond Reafon, Brother?

Anf. There were but Eleven Apoftles when *Judas* betrayed Chrift.

Maf. What Form is your Lodge?

Anf. An oblong Square.

Maf. How long, Brother?

Anf. From Eaft to Weft.

Maf. How wide, Brother?

Anf. Between North and South?

Maf. How high, Brother?

Anf. From the Earth to the Heavens.

Maf. How deep, Brother?

Anf. From the Surface of the Earth to the Centre.

Maf. Why is your Lodge faid to be from the Surface to the Centre of the Earth?

Anf. Becaufe that Mafonry is univerfal.

Maf. Why is your Lodge fituate Eaft and Weft?

Anf. Becaufe all Churches or Chapels are or ought to be fo.

Maf. Why fo, Brother?

Anf. Becaufe the Gofpel was firft preached in the Eaft, and extended itfelf to the Weft.

Maf. What fupports your Lodge?

Anf. Three great Pillars.

Maf. What are their Names?

Anf. Wifdom, Strength, and Beauty.

Maf. Who doth the Pillar of Wifdom reprefent?

Anf. The Mafter in the Eaft.

Maf. Who doth the Pillar of Beauty reprefent?

Anf.

Anf. The Junior Warden in the South.

Maf. Why fhould the Mafter reprefent the Pillar of Wifdom ?

Anf. Becaufe he gives Inftructions to the Crafts to carry on their work in a proper manner, with good Harmony.

Maf. Why fhould the Senior Warden reprefent the Pillar of Strength?

Anf. As the Sun fets to finifh the Day, fo the Senior Warden ftands in the Weft to pay the Hirelings their Wages, which is the Strength and Support of all Bufinefs.

Maf. Why fhould the Junior Warden reprefent the Pillar of Beauty?

Anf. Becaufe he ftands in the South at high Twelve at Noon, which is the Beauty of the Day, to call the Men off from Work to Refrefhment, and to fee that they come on again in due time, that the Mafter may have Pleafure and Profit therein.

Maf. Why is it faid that your Lodge is fupported by thofe three great Pillars, Wifdom, Strength, and Beauty?

Anf. Becaufe Wifdom, Strength, and Beauty is the Finifher of all Works, and nothing can be carried on without them.

Maf. Why fo, Brother?

Anf. Becaufe there is Wifdom to contrive, Strength to fupport, and Beauty to adorn.

Maf. Had you any Covering to your Lodge?

Anf. Yes, a clouded Canopy of divers Colours.

Maf. How blows a Mafon's Wind, Brother?

Anf. Due Eaft and Weft.

Maf. What is it o'Clock, Brother? *Anf.* High Twelve.

Maf. Call the Men off from Work to Refrefhment, and fee that they come on again in due Time.

[The Entered Apprentice's Lecture being finifhed, it is cuftomary for the Mafter to call upon one of the Brethren, who can beft acquit himfelf, for the following Song, which is always readily complied with.]

SONG, *At the Conclufion of the Entered Apprentice's* LECTURE.

 COME, let us prepare,
  We Brothers that are,
Affembled on every Occafion ;
 Let us drink, laugh, and fing,
 Our Wine has a Spring ;
Here's a Health to an Accepted Mafon.
    Chorus. Let's drink, &c.
 The world is in Pain,
 Our Secrets to gain,
And ftill let them wonder and gaze on !

   D   They

(20)

They ne'er can divine,
The Word or the Sign
Of a free and an Accepted Mafon.
'Tis this, and 'tis that,
They cannot tell what,
Why fo many great Men of the Nation,
Should Aprons put on,
To make themfelves one,
With a Free and an accepted Mafon.
Great Kings, Dukes, and Lords,
Have laid by their Swords,
Our Myft'ry to put a good Grace on;
And ne'er been afham'd
To hear themfelves nam'd,
With a Free and an Accepted Mafon.
Antiquity's Pride,
We have on our fide,
And it maketh Men juft in their Station;
There's nought but what's good,
To be underftood,
By a Free and an Accepted Mafon.
We're true and fincere,
And juft to the Fair,
Who will truft us on every Occafion;
No mortal can more
The Ladies adore,
Than a Free and an Accepted Mafon.
Then join Hand and Hand,
T'each other firm ftand,
Let's be merry, and put a bright Face on;
What Mortal can boaft,
So noble a Toaft,
As a Free and an Accepted Mafon?

While this Song is finging, they all ftand round the Table, and when they come to the laft Verfe they join Hands crofs-ways in the following Manner: The Right Hand Man takes hold of the Left Hand of his Neighbour with his Right Hand; and the Left Hand Man takes hold of the Right Hand of his next Brother with his Left Hand, fo as to form a Chain by fo many Links, and all join in the Chorus, jumping violently with their Feet on the Floor, and fhaking their Hands up and down, linked together as above, keeping exaÉt time with both.

Every one now talks of what he pleafes, and as it is generally half an Hour before they proceed to Bufinefs, thofe who per-haps have ordered a Supper retire into another Room; but before

(21)

fore they are permitted, the Mafter proceeds *to call the Men off from work*, as it is termed, which is done in this Manner: The Mafter whifpers to the Senior Deacon, who fits on his Right Hand, and fays, " It is high time to call the men from Work to refrefh themfelves :" The Senior Deacon whifpers it to the Senior Warden ; and it is communicated from him to the Junior Deacon, who carries it to the Junior Warden ; he proclaims it openly to the Lodge, and fets his Column upright*, and the Senior Warden lays his down, which fignifies that the Junior Warden is intrufted with the C- e of the Lodge, while the Brethren refrefh themfelves.

In this place it will be neceffary to acquaint the Reader how he may difcover an Entered Apprentice by drinking with him in company. Take the Glafs with your Right Hand, and draw it acrofs your Throat, either before or after you drink ; and if an Apprentice is prefent, he will immediately take Notice of it, by afking you fome Queftion in Mafonry, which you will readily anfwer from this Book. If he afks you the meaning of your doing that, you may whifper to him, that it is the Penalty of the Obligation of an Entered Apprentice. From this Anfwer he will proceed farther in his inquiry.

The Brethren having now regaled themfelves, they take their Seats, and the Mafter proceeds to fet them on again, which is performed in the fame manner as the calling off ; with this Difference, the Warden proclaims, " It is our " Worfhipful Mafter's Pleafure that this Lodge is called " from Refrefhment to Work." The Junior Warden lays down his Column, and the Senior fets his up. But as it often happens that the Time will not permit for the Fellow-Craft's Lecture, they clofe the Lodge, which is done after the fame Manner as that of opening. The Senior Warden declares it in the following Words : " It is our Mafter's " Will and Pleafure, that this Lodge ftand clofed till the " Firft or Third Wednefday in the next Month," according to the Night the Lodge is held. Then the Mafter, Wardens, Deacons, Secretary, &c. take off the Enfigns and Ornaments from their necks, and every one is at Liberty to depart or ftay longer ; every thing of Mafonry is excluded ; they talk of what they pleafe, and fing various Songs for their Amufement.

I fhall now proceed to the Second Degree of Mafonry, called the *Fellow Craft*'s : that is, one who has ferved his Time juftly and lawfully as an Entered Apprentice ; and defires to

---

* The Senior and Junior Warden's Columns are about twenty-five Inches long, and reprefent the Columns that fupport the Porch of *Solomon*'s Temple; The Senior's is called JACHIN, and fignifies *Strength* ; the Junior's BOAZ, and fignifies, *to eftablifh in the Lord*. See the Firft Book of Kings, Chap. VII.

D 2   become

(22)

become more perfect in Mafonry, by being admitted a Fellow Craft. But in moſt Lodges at this Time, they are
made Entered Apprentices and Fellow Craft the ſame
Evening. The Ceremony is the ſame, though they have
different Lectures, Paſs-Word, and Grip belonging to each.

The Fellow-Craft's Lecture.

Maſ. **B**ROTHER, are you a Fellow-Craft?
    Anſ. I am. Try me, prove me.
Maſ. Where was you made a Fellow-Craft?
Anſ. In a juſt and lawful Lodge.
Maſ. How was you prepared to be made a Fellow-Craft?
Anſ. I was neither naked nor cloathed, bare-foot, nor ſhod;
in a halting moving Poſture; deprived of all Metal, I was led
to the Door of the Lodge by the Hand of a Brother.
Maſ. How got you Admittance?
Anſ. By three diſtinct Knocks.
Maſ. What was ſaid to you within?
Anſ. Who comes there?
Maſ. Your Anſwer, Brother?
Anſ. One who has ſerved his Time juſtly and lawfully
as an Entered Apprentice, and now begs to become more
perfect in Mafonry, by being admitted a Fellow-Craft.
Maſ. How do you expect to attain to this Degree?
Anſ. By the Benefit of a Paſs-Word.
Maſ. Have you got that Paſs-word?
Anſ. I have.
Maſ. Give it me, Brother?
Anſ. SHIBBOLETH*.
Maſ. What did he then ſay to you?
Anſ. Paſs, *Shibboleth.*
Maſ. What became of you then?
Anſ. I was led twice round the Lodge.
Maſ. Where did you meet with the firſt Oppoſition?
Anſ. At the Back of the Senior Warden.
Maſ. Where did you meet with the Second Oppoſition?
Anſ. At the Back of the Maſter, where I repeated the ſame
as before.
Maſ. What did he do with you?
Anſ. He ordered me back to the Senior Warden to receive
Inſtructions.
Maſ. What Inſtructions did he give you?
Anſ. He taught me to ſhew the Maſter my due Guard,
and to take two Steps upon the ſecond Step of a Right An-
gled Oblong Square, with my Right Knee bent bare, my

* SHIBBOLETH, the Paſs-word of a Fellow-Craft; ſignifies *Plenty.* See
the xiith Chapter of the Book of Judges.

2

Left

Left Foot forming a Square, my Body upright, my Right Hand on the Holy Bible, my left Arm supported by the Points of the Compasses, forming a Square, where I took the Obligation of a Fellow-Craft.

Maf. Have you got that Obligation, Brother?

Anf. I have, Right Worshipful.

Maf. Can you repeat it ?

Anf. I'll do my Endeavour, Right Worshipful, with your Affiftance.

Maf. Pray ftand up, and let the Brethren hear it.

The Obligation of a Fellow-craft

" I——*A. B.* of my own Free Will and ..ccord, and in
" the Prefence of Almighty God, and this Right Worshipful
" Lodge, dedicated to St. *John*, do hereby fwear, that I
" will always hale, conceal, and never reveal, that Part of
" a Fellow-Craft to an Entered Apprentice, or either of
" them, except it be in a true and lawful Lodge of Crafts,
" him or them whom I fhall find to be fuch, after juft Trial
" and Examination.—I do furthermore fwear, that I will
" anfwer all Signs and Summonfes fent to me from a Lodge
" of Crafts, within the Length of a Cable-Tow*. I alfo
" fwear, that I will not wrong a Brother, nor fee him
" wronged, but give him timely Notice of all approaching
" Dangers whatfoever, as far as in me is. I will alfo ferve
" a Brother as much as lies in my Power, without being
" detrimental to myfelf or Family : and I will keep all my
" Brother's Secrets as my own, that fhall be delivered to
" me as fuch, Murder and Treafon excepted. All this I
" fwear, with a firm and fteady Refolution to perform the
" fame, without any Equivocation or Hefitation in me
" whatfoever, under no lefs Penalty than to have my Heart
" torn from my naked left Breaft, and given to the Vultures
" of the Air as a Prey. So help me God, and keep me ftedfaft
" in this my Fellow-Craft's Obligation. [*Kiffes the book.*]

Maf. Thank you, Brother.—After you received this Obligation, pray what was fhewn to you?

Anf. The Sign of a Fellow-Craft.

Maf. Pray give it me. *Anf.* I will, Right Worshipful.
[He ftands up, and puts his Right Hand to his Left Breaft, keeping his Thumb fquare ; and his Left Hand raifed up, fo as to form a fquare.]

Maf. What was the next Thing done to you?

Anf. He took me by the Right Hand, and gave me the Grip and Word of a Fellow-Craft, and the Pafs Grip†.

* A Cable Tow is three Miles in Length ; fo that if a Fellow-Craft is at that Diftance from his Lodge, he is not culpable on account of his Non-Attendance.

† The Pafs-Grip is thus performed: You muft put your Thumb-Nail betwe:n

Maf. What did they then to you?

Anf. He took me by the Right Hand, and faid Rife, Brother *Boaz.*

Maf. What followed after that, Brother?

Anf. He ordered me back, when every Thing I had been diveſted of was reſtored, and I was brought in again in order to return Thanks*.

Maf. Being thus admitted, Brother, did you ever work as a Craft?

Anf. Yes, Right Worſhipful, in building the Temple.

Maf. Where did you receive your wages?

Anf. In the Middle Chamber.

Maf. When you came to the Door of the Middle Chamber, pray who did you fee?   *Anf.* A Warden.

Maf. What did he demand of you?

Anf. The Paſs-word of a Fellow-Craft.

Maf. Did you give it him?   *Anf.* I did, Right Worſhipful.

Maf. Pray what is it?   *Anf.* SHIBBOLETH.

Maf. How got you to the Middle Chamber?

Anf. Through the Porch.

Maf. Did you fee any Thing worth you Notice?

Anf. I did, Right Worſhipful.

Maf. What was it?   *Anf.* Two fine Braſs Pillars.

Maf. What are their Names?

Anf. JACHIN and BOAZ.

Maf. How high were theſe Pillars?

Anf. Thirty-five Cubits, with a Chapiter Five Cubits †, which made it Forty in the whole.

[This is deſcribed more clearly in the Third Chapter of the Second Book of Chronicles, Verſe 15th.]

Maf. What were they ornamented with, Brother?

Anf. Two Chapiters, each Five Cubits in Height.

Maf. What were they adorned with beſides?

Anf. Lilly-work, Net-work, and Pomegranates.

Maf. Were they hollow, Brother?

Anf. Yes, Right Worſhipful.

Maf. How thick was the outſide Coat? *Anf.* Four Inches.

Maf. Where were they caſt?

between the Firſt and Second Joint of the Right Hand, and whiſper the Word SHIBBOLETH. The Grip of a Fellow-Craft is by putting the Thumb-Nail on the Second Joint of the Right Hand, and the Word is BOAZ.
* The Ceremony of returning Thanks is the fame as the Entered Apprentice's, excepting *for admitting me a Fellow-Craft.*
† The Reader is here to underſtand that there are three Sorts of Cubits; the King's Cubit, three Engliſh Feet; the Holy Cubit, one Foot ſix Inches; and the common Cubit, twenty one Inches. The Cubit mentioned in the Old Teſtament is the Holy Cubit, which is one Foot ſix Inches.

Anf.

Anf. On the Plain of *Jordan*, between *Succoth* and *Zartha*, in a Clay Ground, where all *Solomon*'s holy Veffels were caft.

Maf. Who caft them, Brother?

Anf. Hiram *Abiff*, the Widow's Son.

This generally finifhes the Fellow-Craft's Lecture, and very few Lodges go fo far in their Queftions and Anfwers: Therefore, in order to enliven the Company, the Mafter afks fome good Singer to favour them with the following Song, which I have heard fung with great Energy and Rapture throughout the Lodge; every Brother bearing a Part in the Chorus.

The FELLOW-CRAFT's SONG.

HAIL, Mafonry! thou Craft divine!
  Glory of Earth, from Heaven reveal'd,
Which does with Jewels precious fhine,
  From all but Mafon's eyes conceal'd.
Chorus. Thy praifes due who can rehearfe,
   In nervous profe, or flowing Verfe?

As Men from Brutes diftinguifh'd are,
  A Mafon other Men excels,
For what's in Knowledge choice or rare,
  But in his Breaft fecurely dwells.
Chorus. His filent Breaft and faithful Heart.
   Preferve the Secrets of the Art.

From fcorching Heat and piercing Cold,
  From Beafts whofe roar the Foreft rends;
From the Affaults of Warriors bold,
  The Mafon's Art Mankind defends.
Chorus. Be to this Art due Honour paid,
   From which Mankind receives fuch Aid.

Enfigns of State that feed our Pride,
  Diftinctions troublefome and vain,
By Mafon's true are laid afide.
  Art's free-born Sons fuch Toys difdain.
Chorus. Ennobled by the Name they bear,
   Diftinguifh'd by the Badge* they wear.

Sweet Fellowfhip, from Envy free,
  Friendly Converfe of Brotherhood!
The Lodge's lafting Cement be,
  Which has for Ages firmly ftood.
Chorus. A Lodge thus built for Ages paft,
   Has lafted, and will ever laft.

* Here the whole Lodge ftrike their Right Hands all at once on their Aprons, keeping as regular Time as the Soldiers in *St. James's Park*, when they ftrike their Cartouch Boxes.

Then

(26)

Then in our Songs be Juſtice done,
To thoſe who have enrich'd the Art,
From *Jabel* down to *Aberdour**
And let each Brother bear a Part.
Chorus. Let noble Maſons Healths go round,
Their praiſe in lofty Lodge reſound.

In Company the Fellow-Craft takes the Pot or Glaſs, and draws it acroſs his left Breaſt, and touches it; the Penalty being this, that he would ſooner have his Heart torn from his Left Breaſt, and given to the Fowls of the Air, than diſcover the Secrets of Maſonry. Sometimes this is done with the Right Hand only, as it is leſs taken Notice of by Strangers.

Having given the Entered Apprentice and Fellow-Craft's Part, I now proceed to the third and laſt Degree of Maſonry, which is termed *the Maſter's Part*, it being performed in the ſame Manner as the other two, *viz.* by Way of Queſtion and Anſwer, and is as follows:

Maſ. **B**ROTHER, where have you been?
    Anſ. In the Weſt.
Maſ. And where are you going?   *Anſ.* To the Eaſt.
Maſ. Why do you leave the Weſt, and go to the Eaſt?
Anſ. Becauſe the Light of the Goſpel was firſt ſhewn in the Eaſt?
Maſ. What are you going to do in the Eaſt?
Anſ. To ſeek for a Lodge of Maſters.

* Lord *Aberdour* was formerly Grand Maſter; at preſent Lord *Petre* fills that Station; and they make uſe of his Name accordingly. For the Entertainment of our Readers, the Editor obtained a complete Liſt of all the Grand Maſters, ſince the Year 1722, viz.

Francis Scott, Earl of Dalkeith,
Charles Lenox, Duke of Richmond Lenox and Aubigny,
J. Hamilton, Lord Paiſley,
Wm. O'Brien, Earl of Inchiquin,
Henry Hare, Lord Colraine,
James King, Lord Kingſton,
Tho. Howard, Duke of Norfolk,
T. Coke, Lord Lovell,
Ant. Brown, Ld. Viſc. Montacute,
James Lyon, Earl of Strathmore,
John Lindſey, Earl of Crauford,
Thomas Thynne, Lord Viſcount Weymouth,
John Campbell, Earl of Loudon,

Edward Bligh, Earl of Darnley,
H. Brydges, Marq. of Caernarvon,
Rob. Raymond, Lord Raymond,
John Keith, Earl of Kintore,
J. Douglas, Earl of Morton,
John Ward, Lord Ward,
Tho. Lyon, Earl of Strathmore,
James Cranſtoun, Lord Cranſtoun,
Wm. Byron, Lord Byron,
John Proby, Lord Caryſfort,
James Brydges, E. of Caernarvon,
Sholto Ch. Douglas, Lord Aberdour,
W. Shirley, Lord Ferrers, and the preſent Lord Petre.

By the above noble Liſt of Grand Maſters, ſuch as no Age, Society, or Kingdom could ever boaſt to have ruled them, Maſonry has been fixed on the ſolid Baſis it now ſtands.

                                                                Maſ.

(27)

Maſ. Then you are a Maſter Maſon, I preſume?
Anſ. I am ſo taken and accepted among Maſters?
Maſ. Where was you made Maſter?
Anſ. In a Lodge of Maſters.
Maſ. How was you prepared to be made Maſter?
Anſ. My Shoes were taken off my Feet, my Arms and Breaſt were naked, and I was deprived of all Metal. In this Manner I was led to the Door of the Lodge*.
Maſ. How got you Admittance?
Anſ. By three diſtinct Knocks.
Maſ. What was then ſaid to you from within?
Anſ. Who comes there?
Maſ. Your Anſwer, Brother?
Anſ. One who hath lawfully and truly ſerved his Time as an Entered Apprentice and Fellow-Craft, and now begs to attain the laſt and moſt honourable Degree of Maſonry, by being admitted a Maſter.
Maſ. How do you expect to attain it?
Anſ. By the Benefit of a Paſs-Word.
Maſ. Can you give me that Word, Brother?
Anſ. I can and will, Right Worſhipful.
Maſ. Pray give it me then.   *Anſ.* TUBAL CAIN†.
Maſ. What was then ſaid to you?
Anſ. Enter TUBAL CAIN.
Maſ. How was you diſpoſed of?
Anſ. I was led round the Lodge.
Maſ. Where did you meet with the firſt Oppoſition?
Anſ. At the Back of the Maſter.
Maſ. What did he demand of you?
Anſ. The ſame as at the Door.
Maſ. How did he diſpoſe of you?
Anſ. He ordered me back to the Senior Warden, in the Weſt, to receive proper Inſtructions.
Maſ. What were thoſe Inſtructions, Brother?
Anſ. He inſtructed me as I ſtood in the Weſt, *Firſt*, To ſhew the Maſter in the Eaſt the due Guard or Sign of an Entered Apprentice, and take one Step upon the Firſt Step of the Right Angle of an Oblong Square, with my Left

---

* The Difference between the Manner of preparing the Perſon for the Degree of Maſter and the Entered Apprentice and Fellow-Craft, is this: That the Entered Apprentice's Left Arm and Left Breaſt is naked, with the Left Shoe off; and the Fellow-Craft's Right Breaſt is naked, with the Right Shoe off.

† TUBAL CAIN was the firſt Perſon who made uſe of Braſs, Iron, and other Metals, and is ſaid to be the Inventor of Muſic. His Deſcent was from the fifth Generation of *Cain.* In Scripture it is ſaid he became famous in working Metals, which *Hiram* afterwards greatly improved.

E   Foot

(28)

Foot forming a Square. *Secondly*, To make two Steps upon the fame Oblong Square, and to fhew the Sign of a Fellow-Craft. *Thirdl*:, I was taught to take two Steps upon the fame Oblong Square, with both my Knees bent, and bare; my Body upright, my Right-Hand upon the Holy Bible, both Points of a Pair Compaffes being pointed to my Right and Left Breaft, where I took the folemn Oath or Obligation of a Mafter-Mafon.

Maf. Brother, can you remember the Obligation you fpeak of?

Anf. I'll do my endeavour, Right Worfhipful, with your Affiftance.

Maf. Pray ftand up, and begin.

Anf. " I *A. B.* of my own Free Will and Accord, and in
" the Prefence of Almighty God, and this Right Worfhipful
" Lodge, dedicated to Holy St. *John*, do hereby and hereon
" moft folemnly and fincerely fwear, that I will always hale,
" conceal, and never reveal, this Part of a Mafter Mafon to
" a Fellow-Craft, any more than that of a Fellow-Craft to
" an Apprentice, or any of them to the reft of the World,
" except in a true and lawful Lodge of Mafters, him or them
" whom I fhall find to be fuch, after a juft Trial and Exami-
" nation.——I furthermore do fwear, that I will attend all
" Summonfes fent to me from a Lodge of Mafters, if within
" the Length of a Cable-Tow.—I will alfo keep all my Bro-
" thers Secrets as my own, Treafon and Murder excepted,
" and that at my own Free Will.—I will not wrong a Bro-
" ther, or fee him wronged, but give him Notice of all Dan-
" ger, as far as in my power lies.—And I alfo fwear, that
" I will conform myfelf to all the Laws and Inftitutions of
" this Lodge.—All this I fwear, with a firm and fixed Refo-
" lution to perform the fame, under no lefs Penalty than to
" have my Body fevered in two; the one Part carried to the
" South, the other to the North; my Bowels burnt to Afhes,
" and the Afhes to be fcattered to the four Winds of the
" Heavens, that no further Remembrance of fuch a vile
" Wretch may exift among Men (and in particular Mafons.)
" So help me God, and keep me ftedfaft in this my Mafter's
" Obligation." [*Kiffes the Book.*]

Maf. Thank you, Brother.——Pray what was fhewn you after you had received this Obligation?

Anf. One of the Mafter's Signs.

   [This Sign is given by drawing your Right-Hand acrofs
    your Belly, which is the Penalty of the Obligation.
    Then he gives the Mafter the Grip of an Apprentice,
    who fays, What's this? The Perfon anfwers, The Grip
    of an Entered Apprentice.]

Maf.

Maf. Has it got a Name?
Anf. It has, Right Worfhipful.
Maf. Will you give it me?
Anf. JACHIN.
Maf. Will you be of or from?   *Anf.* From.
Maf. From what, Brother?
Anf. From an Entered Apprentice to a Fellow-Craft.
Maf. Pafs, Brother.
[He puts his Thumb between the firft and fecond Joint,
which is the Pafs-Grip, and you pronounce the Word
SHIBBOLETH.]
Maf. What was done to you after that?
Anf. He took me by the Grip of a Fellow-Craft, and faid,
What's this?
Maf. Your Anfwer, Brother?
Anf. The Grip of a Fellow-Craft.
Maf. Has it got a Name?   *Anf.* It has.
Maf. Will you give it me?   *Anf.* BOAZ.
Maf. What was then faid to you?
Anf. Rife up, Brother BOAZ.
Maf. Brother, what followed?
Anf. He told me I reprefented one of the greateft men in
the World, *viz.* our Grand Mafter *Hiram*, who was killed
juft at the finifhing of the Temple; and the Manner of his
Death is thus related:

" There were originally fifteen Fellow-Crafts, who per-
ceiving the Temple almoft finifhed, and not having received
the Mafter's Word, they grew impatient, and agreed to extort
it from their Mafter *Hiram* the firft Opportunity they could
find of meeting him alone, that they might pafs for Mafters
in other Countries, and receive the Wages or Profits of Mafters; but before they could accomplifh their Scheme, twelve
of them recanted; the other three were obftinate, and deter-
mined to have it by Force, if no other Way could be found:
their Names were, *Jubela*, *Jubelo*, and *Jubelum*.

" It being always the Cuftom of *Hiram*, at Twelve at
Noon, as foon as the Men were called off to refrefh themfelves, to go into the *Sanctum Sanctorum*, or Holy of Holies,
to pay his Devotion to the true and living God, the three
Affaffins above-mentioned placed themfelves at the Eaft,
Weft, and South Doors of the Temple. At the North there
was no Entrance, becaufe the Rays of the Sun never dart
from that Point.

" *Hiram*, having finifhed his Prayer to the Lord, came
to the Eaft Door, which he found guarded by *Jubela*, who
demanded the Mafter's Grip in a refolute Manner; he received for anfwer from *Hiram*, that it was not cuftomary
E 2   to

(30)

to afk it in fuch a Strain; that he himfelf did not receive it fo; adding, that he muft wait, and Time and Patience would bri: it about. He told him farther, that it was not in his Power alone to reveal it, except in the Prefence of *Solomon* King of *Ifrael*, and *Hiram* King of *Tyre*. *Jubela* being diffatisfied with this Anfwer, ftruck him acrofs the Throat with a twenty-four Inch Gauge. *Hiram* upon this Ufage flew to the South Door of the Temple, where he was met by *Jubelo*, who afked him the Mafter's Grip and Word in like Manner as *Jubela* had done before; and on receiving the fame Anfwer from his Mafter, he gave him a violent Blow with a Square upon his Left Breaft, which made him reel. Upon recovering his Strength, he ran to the Weft Door, the only Way left him of efcaping; and on being interrogated by *Jubelum* to the fame Purport, who guarded that Paffage, (to whom he replied as at firft) he received a terrible Fracture upon his Head with a Gavel[a] or Setting Maul, which occafioned his Death. After this they carried his Body out at the Weft Door[+], and hid it under fome Rubbifh till Twelvo

* When you come to this Part of the Ceremony of making a Mafter, it occafionar fome Surprife; the Junior Warden ftrikes you with a twenty-four Inch Gauge acrofs your Throat; the Senior Warden follows the Blow, by ftriking you with a Square on the Left Breaft; and almoft at the fame Inftant the Mafter knocks you down with the Gavel. This is the Cuftom in moft Lodges; and it requires no fmall Shaie of Courage, for the Blows are frequently fo fevere that the poor Candidate falls backwards on the Floor; and the greater h's Terror at this Ufage, the more the Brethren are pleafed. This Cuftom favours too much of Barbarity; and many Inftances can be produced of Perfons in this Situation, who have requefted on their Knees to be fet at Liberty, and others who have made their Efcape as faft as poffible out of the Lodge. The *French* and Natives of *Switzerland* have a more ftriking and folemn Way of reprefenting the Death of *Hiram*. When a Brother comes into the Lodge, in order to be raifed to the Degree of Mafter, one of the Members lies flat on his Back, with his Face difigured, and befmeared with Blood, on the Spot where the Drawing on the Floor is made. His natural Surprife and Confufion immediately appears, and one of the Brethren generally addreffes him to the Purport following: " Brother, be not " frightened; this is the unfortunate Remains of a Worthy Mafter, that " would not deliver the Grip and Word to three Fellow-Crafts, who had " no Right to it; and from this Example we learn our Duty, viz. to die " before we deliver the Mafter's Part of Mafonry to thofe who have no " Claim thereto." On kneeling to receive the Obligation, the fuppofed dead Brother lies behind you, and during the Time of adminiftering the Oath, and reading the Hiftory of his Death, he gets up, and you are laid down in his Place. This is the moft material Difference between the *French* and *Englifh* Method of making a Mafter Mafon: and that it is more agreeable to Humanity than giving a Man a violent Blow on the Forehead with a Gavel, muft be obvious to every Reader.

† In this Point the Mafons themfelves differ: fome of them fay, he was not carried out at the Weft Door, but buried on the Spot where he was killed in this Manner: The three Affaffins took up Part of the Pavement, made a Hole, and covered him over with Stones as foon as they had crammed him in; after which they conveyed the Rubbifh out in their Aprons, to prevent Sufpicion.

o'Clock

(31)

o'Clock the next Night, when they met by Agreement; and buried him on the Side of a Hill, in a Grave six Feet perpendicular, dug due East and West.

Maf. After you was thus knocked down, what was said to you then?

Anf. I was told I reprefented one of the greateft men in the World lying dead, *viz.* our Grand Mafter *Hiram.*

Maf. Thank you, Brother.—Pray go on.

Anf. As I lay on my Back, the Mafter informed me how *Hiram* was found; and by what means the three Ruffians were difcovered, as follows:

" Our Mafter *Hiram* not coming to view the Workmen as ufual, King *Solomon* caufed ftrict Search to be made; but this proving ineffectual, he was fuppofed to be dead. The Twelve Fellow-Crafts who recanted, hearing the Report, their Confciences pricking them, went to *Solomon* with white Aprons and Gloves, Emblems of their Innocence, and informed him of every Thing relative to the Affair, as far as they knew, and offered their Affiftance in order to difcover the three other Fellow-Crafts who had abfconded. They feparated, and divided themfelves into four Parties; three Eaft, Weft, North, and South, in Queft of the Murderers. As one of the Twelve was travelling on the Sea-fide, near *Joppa,* being fatigued, he fat down to refrefh himfelf: but was foon alarmed by the following hideous Exclamations from the Cliff of a Rock: " Oh! that my Throat had been cut
" acrofs, my Tongue torn out by the Root, and buried in
" the Sands of the Sea at Low-water Mark, a Cable's Length
" from the Shore, where the Tide ebbs and flows twice in
" Twenty-four Hours, e'er I had confented to the Death of
" our Grand Mafter *Hiram!*"—" Oh! (fays another) that
" my Heart had been torn from under my naked Left Breaft,
" and given a Prey to the Vultures of the Air, rather than I
" had been concerned in the Death of fo good a Mafter!"
" But (fays a third) I ftruck him harder than you both;
" 'twas I that killed him. Oh! that my Body had been fever-
" ed in two, and fcattered to the South and North; my Bow-
" els burnt to Afhes in the South, and fcattered between the
" four Winds of the Earth, ere I had been the caufe of the
" Death of our good Mafter *Hiram!*" The Fellow-Craft hearing this, went in Queft of his two Affociates, and they entered the Cliff of the Rock, took and bound them faft, and brought them to King *Solomon,* before whom they voluntarily confeffed their Guilt, and begged to die. The Sentence paffed on them was the fame as they expreffed in their Lamentation in the Cliff; *Jubela*'s Throat was cut acrofs; *Jubelo*'s Heart was torn from under his Left Breaft; and *Jubelum*'s Body was fevered in two, and fcattered in the South and North.

" When

128

(32)

" When the Execution was over, King *Solomon* fent for the Twelve Crafts, and defired them to take the Body of *Hiram* up, in order that it might be interred in a folemn Manner in the *Sanctum Sanctorum*; he alfo told them, that if they could not find a Key-Word about him, it was loft; for there were only three in the World to whom it was known; and unlefs they were prefent it could not be delivered. *Hiram* being dead, it confequently was loft. However, as *Solomon* ordered, they went and cleared the Rubbifh, and found their Mafter in a mangled Condition, having lain fifteen Days; upon which they lifted up their Hands above their Heads in Aftonifhment, and faid, *O Lord, my God!* This being the firft Word and Sign, King *Solomon* adopted it as the grand Sign of a Mafter Mafon, and it is ufed at this Day in all the Lodges of Mafters.

Maf. Brother, when *Hiram* was thus found dead, how was he raifed?

Anf. By the Five Points of Fellowfhip.

Maf. What are thefe five Points of Fellowfhip?

Anf. He was taken by the Entered Apprentice's Grip, and the Skin flipped off. Then he was taken by the Fellow-Craft's Grip, which alfo flipped off; and laftly, by the Mafter's Grip*.

Maf. Brother, it appears you could not have been raifed but by the Five Points of Fellowfhip. Pray explain them.

Anf. Hand in Hand fignifies that I will always put forth my Hand to ferve a Brother as far as in my Power lies.—— Foot to Foot, that I never will be afraid to go a Foot out of my Way to ferve a Brother.——Knee to Knee, that when I pray, I fhould never forget my Brother's Welfare. Breaft to Breaft, to fhew I will keep my Brother's Secrets as my own.—The Left Hand fupporting the Back, that I will always fupport a Brother, as far as I can, without being detrimental to my own Family.

Maf. Thank you, Brother.—But pray, why was you deprived of all Metal?

Anf. Becaufe there was neither Axe, Hammer, nor Sound of any Metal Tool heard in the building the Temple of *Solomon*.

Maf. Why fo, Brother?

---

* The Mafter's Grip is thus performed: you take a Brother with the four Finger Nails of your Right Hand, and prefs clofe into the lower Part of the Wrift of his Right Hand with all your Strength; your Right Foot to his Right Foot, and his Right Knee to your Right Knee; the Right Breaft to that of your Brother, and your Left Hand fupporting his Back. In this Pofition you whifper in his Ear MAHABONE, or, as in the Modern Lodges, MAC BENACH, which is the Mafter's Word.

4

Anf.

(33)

Anf. Becaufe it fhould not be polluted.

Maf. How is it poffible, Brother, that fuch a large Building fhould be carried on without the Ufe or Sound of fome Metal Tool?

Anf. It was prepared in the Foreft of *Lebanon*, and brought down upon proper Carriages, and fet up with wooden Mauls made on Purpofe for the Occafion.

Maf. Why were both your Shoes taken off from your Feet?

Anf. Becaufe the Place I ftood on, when I was made a Mafon, was Holy Ground.

Maf. What fupports our Lodge?   *Anf.* Three Pillars.

Maf. Pray what are their Names, Brother?

Anf. Wifdom, Strength, and Beauty.

Maf. What do they reprefent?

Anf. Three Grand Mafters; *Solomon* King of *Ifrael*; *Hiram*, King of *Tyre*; and *Hiram Abiff*, who was killed by the three Fellow-Crafts.

Maf. Were thefe three Grand Mafters concerned in the building of *Solomon*'s Temple?   *Anf.* They were.

Maf. What was their Bufinefs?

Anf. Solomon found Provifions and Money to pay the Workmen; *Hiram* King of *Tyre* provided Materials for the Building; and *Hiram Abiff* performed or fuperintended the Work.

(*End of the Mafter's Lecture.*)

The Form obferved at the Inftalment of a Mafter, and the other Officers, on St. John's Day.

THEY ar being expired, a proper perfon is fixed on by the Members of every Lodge to prefide over and govern the Societies in the Capacity of Mafter. The Qualifications for this Office are, 1ft, That he muft be regularly and lawfully raifed; 2dly, He ought to be a Man of good Character, and irreproachable in his private Conduct: 3dly, He muft be well verfed in the Laws and Conftitutions of the Order, and ought to be temperate, cool, and quite perfect in going through the before-mentioned Lectures, as all the Queftions are put by him, and he is often obliged to affift the Brethren in making the proper Anfwers*; for every Mafon fitting round the Table anfwers in his Turn, in the fame Manner as Boys at Church faying the Catechifm. This is termed *Working.* For Inftance:

* I have been in a Lodge, where the Mafter was quite ignorant of the common Rules of Grammar; frequently making fuch egregious Blunders, that the Brethren could fcarce refrain from burfting into Laughter; and often embellifhing his Queftions with, " Brethren you have *let a body know as how* " you cannot be raifed but by the Five Points of Fellowfhip, &c. *tell us which* " *they be.*"

Suppofe

(34)

Suppofe a Brother meets another, and afks him if he was at
his Lodge laft Night? He fays, Yes. Well, replied the
other, *Did you work?* that is, did you go through the feveral
Queftions and Anfwers in any of the Lectures?—If any Member cannot, or does not chufe *to work*, when the Queftion is
put, and it comes to his Turn, he gets up, and clapping his
Hand on his Breaft, addreffes himfelf to the Mafter, and begs
to be excufed; then the Left Hand Man anfwers in his Room

The Brethren having chofe a proper Man for this Office,
and he being approved of by the Grand Mafter, they proceed
to the Inftalling him as follows: He kneels down in the
South Part of the Lodge, and the late Mafter gives him the
following Obligation before he refigns the Chair, which he
repeats:

" I—*A. B.* of my own Free Will and Confent, in the Pre-
" fence of Almighty God, and this Right Worfhipful Lodge,
" dedicated to St. *John*, do moft folemnly and fincerely fwear,
" that I will not deliver the Word and Grip belonging to the
" Chair whilft I am Mafter, or at any Time hereafter, except
" it be to a Mafter in the Chair, or a Paft Mafter, him or them
" whom I fhall find to be fuch, after a due Trial and Examina-
" tion.—I alfo fwear, that I will act as Mafter of this Lodge
" till next St *John*'s Day, and fill the Chair every Lodge
" Night, if I am within the Length of my Cable-Tow.—I
" likewife further promife, that I will not wrong this Lodge,
" but act in every Refpect for the good of Mafonry, by be-
" having myfelf agreeable to the reft of my Brethren; and
" maintaining good Order and Regularity in this Lodge, as
" far as lies in my Power. All this I fwear, with a firm and
" ftedfaft Refolution to perform the fame, under no lefs than
" the four following Penalties: My Throat cut acrofs, my
" Tongue torn out, my Heart torn from my Left Breaft, and
" my Body fevered in two. So help me God, and affift me in
" this my Obligation belonging to the Chair."[*Kiffes the Book.*]

The Paft Mafter raifes him up, and takes off the Jewels
and Ribbon from his own Neck, and puts it on the New
Mafter, taking him at the fame Time by the Mafter's Grip,
and whifpering in his Ear the Word CHIBBELUM*; after
which he flips his Hand from the Mafter's Grip to the Elbow, and preffes his Nails in, as is done in the Grip of the
Mafter under the Wrift.

* CHIBBELUM fignifies a worthy Mafon. The Origin of the Words and
Signs among Free Mafons was on this Account: *Hiram* the Chief Artichitect of
the Temple, had fo great a Number of Workmen to pay, that he could not
poffibly know them all; he therefore gave each Degree or Clafs, a particular
Sign and Word, by which he could diftinguifh them more readily, in order to pay
them their different Salaries.

The

(35)

The Senior and Junior Warden, Secretary, &c. receive the Obligation as the Mafter, except the Grip and Word; there being none peculiar to them.

Having now gone through the feveral Degrees and Lectures belonging to the Entered Apprentice, Fellow-Craft, Mafter, and the Manner of Inftalment, I fhall clofe the Work with a few general Directions, dividing them under the following Heads:

I. *A Defcription of the Ornaments worn by the different Officers when affembled in the Lodge, and their proper Places of fitting.*

The MASTER, who fits in the Eaft of the Lodge, has the Rule and Compafs, and Square hanging to a Ribbon round his Neck, and a Black Rod in his Hand, when he opens the Lodge, near Seven Feet high.

The SENIOR WARDEN, fits in the Weft, with a Level hanging by a Ribbon round his Neck, and a Column placed on the Table, about twenty-nine Inches long.

The JUNIOR WARDEN's Place is in the South, with the Plumb Rule hanging by a Ribbon from his Neck, and a Column his Hand.

The SECRETARY wears the Crofs-Pens, hanging in the fame Manner.

The Senior and Junior DEACONS have each a Black Rod, with the Compafs hanging round their Necks; the Senior fits at the Back of the Mafter, or at his Right Hand; the Junior at the Senior Warden's Right Hand.

The PAST-MASTER has the Compaffes and Sun, with a Line of Cords about his Neck.

The TREASURER has a Key hanging from his Neck.

II. *The Manner of giving the Signs of each Degree, and the Word belonging to it, with the Fellow-Craft and Mafter's Clap.*

The Mafter's Sign, Grip, and Word, &c.

The Sign. Draw the Right Hand edgeways acrofs your Belly, which is the Penalty of the Obligation.

The Grip. Take hold of the Right Hand of your Brother with your Right Hand, and prefs the four Finger Nails hard under the Wrift of his Right Hand; put your Right Foot to his Right Foot; your Right Knee to his Right Knee; and his Right Breaft to yours, with your Left Hand fupporting his Back.

The Word is MAHABONE; or, in fome Lodges, MAC-BENACH.

The Paff Word is TUBAL-CAIN.

F

The

(36)

The Master's Clap, is by holding both your Hands above your Head, and striking them down at once upon your Apron, both Feet keeping Time. They assign two Reasons for this Sign, viz. When the twelve Fellow-Crafts saw their Master lie dead, they lifted up their Hands in Surprize, and said, *O Lord our God!* and that when *Solomon* dedicated the Temple to the Lord, he stood up, and lifting up both his Hands, exclaimed, *O Lord my God, great art thou above all Gods.*

The Fellow-Craft's Sign, Grip, Word, and Clap.

Sign. Put your Right Hand to your Left Breast, keeping your Thumb square, and your Left Hand upright, forming a Square.

The Pass-Grip, is by putting the Thumb Nail of your Right Hand between the First and Second Joint of a Brother's Right Hand.

The Pass-Word is SHIB. LTH.

The Grip is the same as the Pass-Grip, except pressing your Thumb Nail on the *second* Joint, instead of between the first and second.

The Word is BOAZ.

The Fellow-Craft's Clap is by forming the Sign of a Craft as above, holding your Left Hand square and upright; then clap your Right and Left Hands together; and afterwards strike your Left Breast with your Right Hand, and from thence give a Slap on your Apron, your Right Foot going at the same Time.

The Entered Apprentice's Sign, Grip, and Word.

The Sign. Draw your Hand across your Throat edgeways. The Penalty of the Obligation being this, that an Apprentice would sooner have his Throat cut than discover the Secrets of Masonry.

The Grip. Take a Brother with your Right Hand, and press hard with your Thumb Nail upon the First Joint of the Fore-Finger of his Right Hand.

The Word. Whisper in his Ear JACHIN.

The Master kneels upon both Knees in the Ceremony of Making.

The Craft kneels with the Right Knee.

The Apprentice with the Left Knee.

III. *The Form observed in Drinking.*

The Table being plentifully stored with Wine and Punch, &c. every Man has a Glass set before him, and fills

2   it

it with what he choofes, and as often as he pleafes. But he muft drink his Glafs in Turn, or at leaft keep the Motion with the Reft. When therefore a public Health is given, the Mafter fills firft, and defires the Brethren to charge their Glaffes; and when this is fuppofed to be done, the Mafter fays, *Brethren, are you all charged?* The Senior and Junior Wardens anfwer, *We are all charged in the South and Weft.* Then they all ftand up, and obferving the Mafter's Motion, (like the Soldier his Right Hand Man) drink their Glaffes off; and if the Mafter propofes the Health or Toaft with *three Times Three Claps*, they throw the Glaffes with the Right Hand at full Length, bringing them acrofs their Throats three Times, and making three Motions to put them down on the Table; at the third they are fet down, (though perhaps fifty in Number) as if it was but one: then raifing their Hands Breaft high, they clap nine Times againft the Right, divided into three Divifions, which is termed *Drinking with three Times three*, and at the End they give a Huzza.

Having at length gone through my Plan, I have nothing further to add than this, that the following is the beft Method for a Stranger to gain Admittance, being what I have often tried in many Places, in order to be fully fatisfied.

As foon as you come to the Door of the Lodge, you will find the Tyler on the Outfide, with a drawn Sword in his Hand, and a white Apron on. Afk him if there is a full Lodge? And tell him you fhould be glad of Admittance as a vifiting Member; taking care to provide yourfelf with a white Leather Apron, which you may fhew him as if by Accident. He will, perhaps, afk you what Degree you are of, and defire a Sign, which you may fhew him with Readinefs, and likewife inform him what Lodge you belong to.

It being contrary to the Rules of the Society that the Tyler fhould admit a Stranger, he will go in, and acquaint the Mafter, that fuch a Perfon (mentioning your Name, and the Lodge you told him you belonged to) craves Admittance. Upon which one of the Wardens will come out to examine you, Draw your Right Hand acrofs your Throat edgeways, and he will fay, " What's that?" Your Anfwer muft be " The due Guard of an Apprentice." Then he will take you by the firft Joint of the Thumb of your Right Hand, and prefs it hard with the Thumb-Nail of the Right Hand, and afk, " What's this?"—You muft immediately anfwer, " The Grip of an Entered Apprentice."—If he is not fully fatisfied with this, he will go further on in this Manner.

Quef. Has it got a Name?—You muft anfwer, " It has." Then he will afk you to give it him.

F 2

Anf.

(38)

Anf. I'll halve it with you.—Begin, fays he.—*Anf.* JA-*Mafon.* CHIN. *Anf.* JACHIN.

Quef. Will you be of or from? *Anf.* From.

Quef. From what? *Anf.* From an Entered Apprentice to a Fellow-Craft. He will then fhift his Thumb from the Apprentice's Grip towards the Fellow-Craft's, and afk, What's this? *Anf.* The Pafs-Word of a Fellow-Craft. Give it me, fays he. Whifper in his Ear SHIBBOLETH. On this he will put his Thumb to the fecond Joint, and fay, What's this? *Anf.* The Grip of a Fellow-Craft. Has it a Name? fays he. *Anf.* It has—Pray give it me. *Anf.* I will letter it, or halve it with you. *Mafon.* I'll letter it with you.—*Anf.* Begin. *Mafon.* No, you begin. *Anf.* B. *Mafon.* O. *Anf.* A. *Mafon.* Z. *Anf.* BOAZ.

What I have here offered being more than fufficient, you will be admitted, and you muft put your Apron on, and take your Seat. If there fhould be a making that Night, you will be perfeƈt in the firft Principles, and know more than one in ten who have been Mafons many Years, and have never read this Book.

If you fhould, after this, chufe to go to a Lodge of Mafters, the Ceremony is the fame as above; but you are interrogated as to the Grip, Pafs-Grip, and Word of a Mafter, which you cannot fail of anfwering by reading the Mafter's Part before mentioned. In all this you muft take care not to betray any Fear, but put on an Air of Affü   ƈe.

The Ceremony obferved at the Free-Mafon. Funerals, according to ancient Cuftom.

No Mafon can be interred with the Formalities of the Order, unlefs by his own efpecial Requeft, communicated to the Mafter of the Lodge of which he died a Member: nor unlefs he had been advanced to the third Degree of Mafonry.

The Mafter of the Lodge, on receiving intelligence of his Death, and being made acquainted with the Day and Hour appointed for his Funeral, is to iffue his Commands for fummoning the Lodge; and immediately to make Application, by the Grand Secretary, to the Deputy Grand Mafter, for a legal Power and Authority to attend the Proceffion, with his Officers and fuch Brethren as he may approve of, properly clothed.

The Difpenfation being obtained, the Mafter may invite as many Lodges as he thinks proper, and the Members of the faid Lodges may accompany their Officers in Form; but the whole Ceremony muft be under the Direƈtion of the Mafter of the Lodge to which the Deceafed belonged; and he, and his Officers, muft be duly honoured and chearfully obeyed on the Occafion.

All

(39)

All the Brethren, who walk in Proceffion, fhould obferve, as much as poffible, an uniformity in their Drefs. Decent Mourning, with white Stockings, Gloves, and Aprons, is moft fuitable and becoming. No Perfon ought to he diftinguifhed with a Jewel, unlefs he is an Officer of one of the Lodges invited to attend in Form, and the Officers of fuch Lodges fhould be ornamented with White Safhes and Hatbands; as alfo the Officers of the Lodge to whom the Difpenfation is granted, who fhould likewife be diftinguifhed with White Rods.

In the Proceffion to the Place of Interment, the different Lodges rank according to their Seniority; the Junior ones preceding. Each Lodge forms one Divifion, and the following Order is obferved:

The Tyler with his Sword;
The Stewards, with White Rods;
The Brethren out of Office, two and two;
The Secretary, with a Roll?
The Treafurer, with his Badge of Office;
Senior and Junior-Wardens, Hand in Hand;
The Paft-Mafter,
The Mafter.
The Lodge to which the deceafed Brother belonged, in the following Order; all the Members having Flowers, or Herbs in their Hands.
The Tyler;
The Stewards;
The Mufic [Drums muffled, and Trumpets covered;]
The Members of the Lodge;
The Secretary and Treafurer;
The Senior and Junior Wardens;
The Paft-Mafter.
The Bible and Book of Conftitutions on a Cufhion, covered with black Cloth, carried by a Member of the Lodge:
The MASTER.
The Chorifters finging an Anthem.
The Clergyman;

Pall Bearers;	The BODY, with the Regalia placed thereon and two Swords croffed.	Pall Bearers;

Chief Mourner;
Affiftant Mourners;
Two Stewards;
A Tyler.

One

(40)

One or two Lodges march, before the Proceffion begins, to the Church-yard, to prevent Confufion, and make the neceffary Preparations. The Brethren are on no Account to defert their Ranks, change their Places, but keep in their different Departments. When the Proceffion arrives at the Gate of the Church-yard, the Lodge to which the deceafed Brother belonged, and all the Reft of the Brethren, muft halt, till the Members of the different Lodges have formed a perfect Circle round the Grave, when an opening is made to receive them. They then march up to the Grave, and the Clergyman, and the Officers of the acting Lodge, taking their Station at the Head of the Grave; with the Chorifters on each Side, and the Mourners at the Foot, the Service is rehearfed, an Anthem fung, and that particular Part of the Ceremony is concluded with the ufual Forms. In returning from the Funeral, the fame Order of Proceffion is to be obferved.

This is the whole of Mafonry in all its Branches; and I defy any Mafon to prove the contrary, being ready to anfwer any Queftion propofed, which muft be carefully fealed up, and directed for R. S. to be left with my Publifher, mentioning the Name and Refidence of every Perfon defiring any farther Information. And as to any anonymous Letters or Threatnings on Account of this Publication, they will be treated with Contempt, let them come from what Quarter they will. I alfo declare, that I will always attend and vifit at the Lodges mentioned in the Introduction, or any others as I have done for fome years paft.

ODES, ANTHEMS, and SONGS, fung in the beft LODGES.

O D E I.

HAIL to the CRAFT! at whofe ferene Command,
The gentle ARTS in glad Obedience ftand:
Hail, facred MASONRY! of Source divine,
Unerring Sov'reign of th' unerring Line,
Whofe Plumb of Truth, with never failing Sway,
Makes the join'd Parts of Symmetry obey:
Whofe magic Stroke makes fell Confufion ceafe,
And to the finifh'd ORDERS gives a Place:
Who rears vaft Structures from the Womb of Earth,
And gives imperial Cities glorious Birth.

To Works of Art HER Merit not confin'd,
SHE regulates the Morals, fquares the Mind;
Corrects with Care the Sallies of the Soul,
And points the Tide of Paffions where to roll:
On Virtue's Tablet marks her moral Rule,
And forms her Lodge an univerfal School,
Where Nature's myftic Laws unfolded ftand,
And Senfe and Science join'd, go Hand in Hand.

O may

(41)

O may her focial Rules inftructive fpread,
Till Truth erect HER long neglected Head!
Till through deceitful Night fhe dart her Ray,
And beam full glorious in the Blaze of Day!
Till Men by virtuous Maxims learn to move,
Till all the peopled World HER Laws approve,
And Adam's Race are bound in Brother's Love.

ODE II.

WAKE the Lute and quiv'ring Strings,
   Myftic Truths Urania brings;
Friendly Vifitant, to thee
We owe the Depths of MASONRY:
Faireft of the Virgin Choir,
Warbling to the Golden Lyre,
Welcome here thy ART prevail:
Hail! divine Urania, hail!
Here in Friendfhip's facred Bower,
The downy wing'd and fmiling Hour,
Mirth invites, and focial Song,
Namelefs Myfteries among:
Crown the Bowl and fill the Glafs,
To every Virtue every Grace,
To the BROTHERHOOD refound
Health, and let it thrice go round.

We reftore the Times of old,
The blooming glorious Age of Gold;
As the new Creation free,
Bleft with gay Euphrofyne!
We with god-like Science talk,
And with fair Aftræa walk;
Innocence adorn the Day,
Brighter than the fmiles of May.
Pour the rofy Wine again,
Wake a louder, louder Strain!
Rapid Zephyrs, as ye fly,
Waft our Voices to the Sky;
While we celebrate the NINE,
And the Wonders of the Trine,
While the ANGELS fing above,
As we below, of PEACE and LOVE.

ANTHEM I.

GRANT us kind Heav'n what we requeft,
   In Mafonry let us be bleft;
Direct us to that happy Place,
Where Friendfhip fmiles on every Face,

Where

(42)

Where Freedom and fweet Innocence
Enlarge the Mind and cheer the Senfe.

Where fcepter'd Reafon from her Throne,
Surveys the LODGE, and makes us one ;
And Harmony's delightful Sway
For ever fheds ambrofial Day ;
    Where we blefs Eden's Pleafure tafte,
    Whilft balmy Joys are our Repaft.

No prying Eye can view us here ;
No Fool or Knave difturb our Cheer ;
Our well-form'd Laws fet Mankind free,
And give Relief to Mifery.
    The Poor opprefs'd with Woe and Grief,
    Gain from our bounteous Hands Relief.

Our LODGE the focial Virtues grace,
And Wifdom's Rules we fondly ace ;
All Nature open to our view,
Points out the Paths we fhould purfue.
    Let us fubfift in lafting Peace,
    And may our Happinefs increafe.

ANTHEM II.

BY Mafon's Art th' afpiring Dome
On ftately Columns fhall arife,
All Climates have their native Home,
    Their god-like Actions reach the Skies.
Heroes and Kings revere their Name,
While Poets fing their lafting Fame.

Great, noble, gen'rous, good, and brave ;
    All Virtues they moft juftly claim ;
Their Deeds fhall live beyond the Grave,
    And thofe unborn their Praife proclaim.
Time fhall their glorious Acts enroll,
While Love and Friendfhip charm the Soul.

SONG I.

[*Tune*, Attic Fire.]
ARISE, and blow thy Trumpet, Fame ;
Free-Mafonry aloud proclaim,
    To Realms and World's unknown ;
Tell them of mighty David's Son,
The ife the matchlefs Solomon,
    Priz'd far above his Throne.

                  The

(43)

The folemn Temple's cloud-cap't Towers,
Th' afpiring Domes are Works of ours,
   By us thofe Piles were rais'd:
Then bid Mankind with Songs advance,
And through th' ethereal vaft Expanfe,
   Let Mafonry be prais'd.

We help the Poor in time of Need,
The Naked clothe, the Hungry feed,
   'Tis our Foundation Stone:
We build upon the nobleft Plan;
For Friendfhip rivets Man to Man; } CHORUS.
   And make us all as One.   } *Three Times.*

Still louder, Fame, thy Trumpet blow;
Let all the diftant Regions know
   Free Mafonry is this:
Almighty Wifdom gave it Birth,
And Heav'n has fix'd it here on Earth,
   A Type of future Blifs.

SONG II.

[*Tune*, Rule Britannia.]

WHEN Earth's Foundation firft was laid,
   By the Almighty Artift's Hand,
'Twas then our perfect, our perfect Laws were made,
   Eftablifh'd by his ftrict Command.
Cho. Hail, myfterious; Hail, glorious Mafonry!
  That makes us ever great and free.

As Man throughout for Shelter fought,
   In Vain from Place to Place did roam,
Until from Heaven, from Heaven he was taught,
   To plan, to build, t- fix his Home.
             Hail, myfterious, &c.

Hence illuftrious rofe our Art,
   And now in beauteous Piles appear;
Which fhall to endlefs, to endlefs Time impart,
   How worthy and how great we are.
             Hail, myfterious, &c.

Nor we lefs fam'd, for ev'ry Tye,
   By which the human Thought is bound;
Love, Truth, and Friendfhip, and Friendfhip focially,
   Join all our Hearts and Hands around.
             Hail, myfterious, &c.

        G   Our

(44)

Our Actions still by Virtue blest,
  And to our Precepts ever true,
The World admiring, admiring shall request
  To learn, and our bright Paths pursue.

                         Hail, mysterious, &c.

SONG III.

[Tune, Goddess of Ease.]

GENIUS of Masonry descend,
  And with thee bring thy spotless Train;
Constant our sacred Rites attend,
  While we adore thy peaceful Reign:
Bring with thee Virtue, brightest Maid,
  Bring Love, bring Truth, and Friendship here,
While social Mirth shall lend her Aid,
  To smooth the wrinkled Brow of Care.

Come, Charity, with Goodness crown'd,
  Encircled in thy heav'nly Robe,
Diffuse thy Blessings all around,
  To ev'ry Corner of the Globe;
See where she comes with Power to bless,
  With open Hand and tender Heart,
Which wounded is at Man's Distress,
  And bleeds at ev'ry human Smart.

Envy may ev'ry Ill devise,
  And Falsehood be thy deadliest Foe,
Though Friendship still shall tow'ring rise,
  And sink thy Adversaries low;
Thy well-built Pile shall long endure,
  Through rolling Years preserve its Prime,
Upon a Rock it stands secure,
  And braves the rude Assaults of Time.

Ye happy few, who here extend
  In perfect Lines from East to West,
With fervent Zeal the Lodge defend,
  And lock its Secrets in each Breast:
Since ye are met upon the Square,
  Bid Love and Friendship jointly reign,
Be Peace and Harmony your Care,
  Nor break the adamantine Chain.

2   Behold

(45)

Behold the Planets how they move,
  Yet keep due Order as they run ;
Then imitate the Stars above,
  And fhine refplendent as the Sun :
That future Mafons when they meet,
  May all our glorious Deeds rehearfe,
An*' fay, their Fathers were fo great,
  That they adorn'd the Univerfe.

SONG IV.

[*Tune*, In Infancy, &c.]

LET Mafonry from Pole to Pole
  Her facred Laws expand,
Far as the mighty Waters roll,
  To wafh remoteft Land :
That Virtue has not left Mankind,
  Her focial Maxims prove,
For ftamp'd upon the Mafon's Mind,
  Are Unity and Love.

Afcending to her native Sky,
  Let Mafonry increafe ;
^ glorious Pillar rais'd on high,
  'ntegrity its Bafe.
  :e adds to Olive Boughs, entwin'd,
  An emblematic Dove,
As ftamp'd upon the Mafon's Mind
  Are Unity and Love.

SONG V.

LET Drunkards boaft the Pow'r of Wine,
  And reel from Side to Side ;
Let Lovers kneel at Beauty's Shrine,
  The Sport of Female Pride :
Be ours the more exalted Part,
To celebrate the Mafon's Art,
  And fpread its Praifes wide.

To Dens and Thickets dark and rude,
  For Shelter Beafts repair ;
With Sticks and Straws the feather'd Brood,
  Sufpend their Nefts in Air :
And Man untaught, as wild as thefe,
Binds up fad Huts with Boughs of Trees,
  And feeds on wretched Fare.

G 2   But

(46)

But Science dawning in his Mind;
   The Quarry he explores;
Induſtry and the Arts combin'd,
   Improv'd all Nature's Stores:
Thus Walls were built and Houſes rear'd,
No Storms nor Tempeſts now are fear'd
   Within his well-fram'd Doors.

When ſtately Palaces ariſe,
   When Columns grace the Hall,
When Tow'rs and Spires ſalute the Skies,
   We owe to Maſons all:
Nor Buildings only do they give,
But teach Men how within to live,
   And yield to Reaſon's Call.

All Party Quarrels they deteſt,
   For Virtue and the Arts,
Lodg'd in each true Maſon's Breaſt,
   Unite and rule their Hearts:
By theſe, while Maſons ſquare their Minds,
The State no better Subjects finds,
   None act more upright Parts.

When Bucks and Albions are forgot,
   Free-Maſons will remain;
Muſhrooms, each Day, ſpring up and rot,
   While Oaks ſtretch o'er the Plain:
Let others quarrel, rant, and roar:
Their noiſy Revels when no more,
   Still Maſonry ſhall reign.
Our Leathern Aprons may compare
   With Garters red or blue;
Princes and Kings our Brothers are:
   May they our Rules purſue:
Then drink Succeſs and Health to all
The Craft around this Earthly Ball,
   May Brethren ſtill prove true.

SONG

143

(47)

SONG VI.

KATE and NED.

ONE Night as Ned crept into Bed,
  Beyond his ufual Hour,
His loving Kate, his conftant Mate,
  Began to fcold and low'r.
You naughty Man where have you been,
  No longer I'll be flighted,
Nor thus at Home will mope and moan,
  While you'r abroad delighted?

I own, dear Kate, 'tis fomewhat late,
  But hear me out with Patience,
All Wives you know, are bound to fhew
  Their Hufbands due Obeifance;
In Truth, dear Kate, 'tis fome what late,
  But put a fmiling Face on,
For I, this Night, am made a bright,
  Free and accepted Mafon.

If this be fo, I pray now fhow
  Some certain Sign or Token,
For Mafons can erect a Plan,
  Or ftop a Breach that's open.
I have a Breach, a huge wide Breach,
  That gives me much Vexation,
This if you ftop, you will o'ertop
  All Mafon's in the Nation.

Then Ned arofe, pull'd off his Clothes,
  Drew out his Line and Level,
He pl 'd his Plum beneath her Bum,
  And brought it to a Bevil;
He took his Gauge, his Nine-Inch Gauge,
  And plac'd it with a floping,
He fix'd his Stones like Inigo Jones,
  And left no Crevice open.

Dear Ned, fays Kate, you've done a Feat,
  A Feat of mighty Wonder,
And as for me, you plainly fee,
  I fairly do knock under.
I'd pawn my Gown, my Robe and Coat,
  My Cardinal with Lace on,
If you each Night would be a bright,
  Free and accepted Mafon.

SONG

144

(48)

SONG VII.

[*Tune*,—God Save the King.]

L ET Mafons Fame refound
   Through all the Nations round,
From Pole to Pole :
See what Felicity,
Harmlefs Simplicity,
Like Electricity,
   Runs through the whole.

Such fweet Variety,
Ne'er had Society
   Ever before :
Faith, Hope, and Charity,
Love and Sincerity,
Without Temerity,
   Charm more and more.

When in the Lodge we're met,
And in due Order fet,
   Happy are we :
Our Works are glorious,
Deeds meritorious,
Never cenforious,
   But great and free.

When Folly's Sons arife,
Mafonry to defpife,
   Scorn all their Spite ;
Laugh at their Ignorance,
Pity their Want of Senfe,
Ne'er let them give Offence,
   Firmer unite.

Mafons have long been free,
And may they ever be
   Great as of Yore :
For many Ages paft,
Mafonry has ftood faft,
And may its Gl es laft
   'Till Time' . more.

New

(49)

New ODE, *written by a Member of the* ALFRED LODGE,
at Oxford, and set to Music by Dr. Fisher, *and performed
at the Dedication of* Free-Masons Hall.
Sung by Messrs. Vernon, Reinhold, Norris, *&c.*

S T R O P H E.

A I R. NORRIS.

WHAT solemn Sounds on holy Sinai rung,
  When heavenly Lyres, by Angel-fingers strung,
Accorded to immortal Lay,
That hymn'd Creation's natal Day !

RECITATIVE, *accompanied.* VERNON.

'Twas when the shouting Sons of Morn
  Bless'd the great omnific Word :——
  " Abash'd, hoarse jarring Atoms heard,
  " Forgot their pealing Strife,
  " And softly crouded into Life,"
When Order, Law, and Harmony were born.

C H O R U S.

The mighty Master's Pencil warm
Trac'd out of each the shadowy Form,
And bade each fair Proportion grace
Smiling Nature's modest Face.

A I R. VERNON.

Heaven's rarest Gifts were seen to join,
To deck a finish'd Form divine,
  And fill the sov'reign Artist's Plan ;
Th' Almighty Image stamp'd the glorious Frame,
And seal'd him with the noblest Name,
  Archetype of Beauty, Man.

A N T I S T R O P H E.
SEMICHORUS and CHORUS.

Ye Spirits pure, that rous'd the tuneful Throng,
And rous'd to Rapture each triumphant Tongue ;
  Again with quick instinctive Fire,
  Each harmonious Lip inspire :
Again bid every vocal Throat
  Dissolve in tender votive Strain !

A I R. VERNON.

Now while yonder white rob'd Train
  Before the mystic Shrine,
  In lowly Adoration join,
Now sweep the living Lyre, and swell the melting Note.

RECITATIVE. REINHOLD.

Yet ere the holy Rites begin
The conscious Shrine within,
  Bid your magic Song impart.

AIR.

(50)

AIR. Reinhold.

How within the wasted Heart
 Shook by Passion's ruthless Power,
 Virtue trimm'd her faded Flower,
To opening Buds of fairest Fruit.
 * *How from majestic Nature's glowing Face*
 She caught each animating Grace,
 And planted there th' immortal Root.

EPODE.

RECITATIVE, *accompanied.* Norris.
Daughter of God's, fair Virtue, if to Thee,
 And thy bright Sister, Universal Love,
Soul of all Good, e'er flow'd the soothing Harmony
 Of pious Gratulation————from above;
To us, thy duteous Votaries, impart
 Presence divine !————

AIR. Mr. Norris.

  The Sons of antique Art.
 In high mysterious Jubilee
  With Pæan loud, and solemn Rite,
  Thy holy Step invite,
  And court thy list'ning Ear,
  To drink the Cadence clear
That swells the choral Symphony.

CHORUS.

To thee, by Foot profane untrod,
Their votive Hands have rear'd the high Abode.

RECITATIVE. Reinhold.

 Here shall your Impulse kind
 Inspire the tranced Mind !

AIR. Reinhold.

And Lips of Truth shall sweetly tell
 What heavenly Deeds befit,
The Soul by Wisdom's Lessons smit:
What Praise he claims, who nobly spurns
 Gay Vanities of Life, and tinsel Joys,
For which unpurged Fancy burns.

CHORUS.

 What Pain he shuns who dares be wise
What Glory wins, who dares excel !

  * *The Lines in Italic were omitted in the Music.*
         OFFICERS

(51)

OFFICERS of the GRAND LODGE of ENGLAND, For the Year 1797.

HIS ROYAL HIGHNESS
GEORGE AUGUSTUS FREDERIC,
PRINCE OF WALES,

Electoral Prince of Brunswick and Lunenburgh; Duke of Cornwall and Rothsay; Earl of Chester and Carrick; Baron of Renfrew; Lord of the Isles; Great Steward of Scotland; Captain General of the Honourable Artillery Company of London; and Knight of the most noble order of the Garter,

GRAND MASTER.

The Right Hon. the EARL of MOIRA, BARON RAWDON, &c. &c. &c.

Acting Grand Master.

Sir PETER PARKER, Bart. *Deputy Grand Master.*
Lieut. Col. GEORGE PORTER. *Senior Grand Warden.*
RICHARD BETTINGHAM, Esq. *Junior Grand Warden.*
JAMES HESELTINE, Esq. *Gr. Treasurer (and P. S. G. W.)*
Mr. WILLIAM WHITE, *Grand Secretary.*
Rev. A. H. ECCLES, *Grand Chaplain.*
THOMAS SANDBY, Esq. *Grand Architect.*
Rev. WILLIAM PETERS, *Grand Portrait Painter.*
Chev. BARTHOLOMEW RUSPINI, *Grand Sword-Bearer.*

N. B. *The Grand Secretary attends at Free-Masons' Hall, on the Business of the Society, on Tuesday and Saturday Evenings.*

PROVINCIAL GRAND MASTERS.

America, North, H. Price, Esq. of Boston.
Antigua, William Jarvis, Esq.
Armenia, Dionysius Manasse.
Austrian Netherlands, the Marquis de Gages of Mons.
Bahama Islands, James Bradford, Esq.
Barbadoes, Hon. William Bishop.
Bengal, Babar, and Orissa, Richard Comyns Birch, Esq.
Berkshire, Arthur Stanhope, Esq.
Bermuda Islands, William Popple, Esq.
Bombay, James Todd, Esq.
Buckingham sh. Sir J. Throgmorton, Bart.
Cambridgshire, Rt Hon. Lord Eardley.
Canada, Sir John Johnson, Bart.
Carolina (S.) John Deas, Esq.
Cheshire, Sir Robert Salusbury Cotton, Brt.
Coast of Coromandel, in the East Indies, John Chamier, Esq.
Cornwal, Sir John St. Aubyn, Bart.
Cumberland, H. Ellison, Esq.
Creek, Cherokee, & Chactaw, Nations, in N. America, William Augustus Bowles, Esq.
Denmark, Norway, &c. Prince Charles, Landgrave of Hesse Cassel.
Derbyshire, Sir J. Borlase Warren, Bart.
Devon, Sir Ch. Warw. Bampfylde, Bt.

Durham, Wm Henry Lambton, Esq.
Essex, George Downing, Esq.
Francfort on Maine, Circles of Upper Rhine, Lower Rhine, and *Franconia,* John Charles Brœmer, Esq.
Georgia, Hon. Noble Jones.
Gibraltar, &c. His Royal Highness Prince Edward.
Grenada, &c. General Rob. Melvill.
Guernsey, Jersey, &c. T. Dobree, Esq.
Hanover, Electorate of, and *British Dominions in Germany,* Prince Charles of Mecklinburg Strelitz.
Hamburgh, Bremen, and *Part of Lower Saxony,* Doctor J. Godfried von Exter.
Hampshire, Col. Sherbone Stewart.
Jamaica, Sir Adam Williamson, K. B.
Kent, Doctor William Perfect.
Lancashire, John Allen, Esq.
Leicester & Nottingham, Ld Rancliffe.
Lincolnshire, Rev. William Peters.
Maryland, Henry Harford, Esq.
Montserrat, William Ryan, Esq.
Naples and *Sicily, kingdoms of,* Duc de Sandemetrio Pignatelli.
Norfolk and City of *Norwich,* Sir Ed. Astley, Baronet.
Northumberland, John Errington, Esq.

H   *Oxford-*

(52)

Oxfordshire, Doctor J. M. Hayes.	*Somersetshire*, John Smith, Esq.
Piedmont, in Italy, Count De Bernez.	*Surrey*, James Meyrick, Esq.
Poland, Count Hulsen, Pal. of Miscislaw.	*Suffolk*, William Middleton, Esq.
Radnor, Charles Marsh, Esq.	*Sussex*, General Samuel Hulse.
Russia, his Excellency John Yelaguine,	*Sumatra*, John Macdonald, Esq.
Senator, &c. to her Imperial Majesty	*Wales, South*, Thomas Wyndham, Esq.
the Empress of Russia.	*Warwickshire*, Thomas Thompson, Esq.
St. Croix, John Ryan, Esq.	*Westmorland*, G. C. Braithwaite, Esq.
Shropshire, Staffordshire, Flintshire,	*Worcestershire*, John Dent, Esq.
Denbigoshire, and Montgomery, Hon.	*Yorkshire*, Richard Slater Milnes, Esq.
and Rev. Francis Henry Egerton.	

Representative of the Grand Lodge of England in *Germany*, Colonel Augustus Graefe, Governor to H. S. H. the Prince of Mecklenburg, at Darmstadt.

GRAND STEWARDS.

For 1796.	For 1797.
Brother Sir John Eamer, President.	Brother R. H. Bradshaw.
L. R. Mackintosh, Treas.	Bailey Heath.
James Duberly, Sec.	John Bullock.
William Veel.	Charles Turner.
Joseph Dennison.	Robert Harper.
Robert Sutton.	T. A. Loxley.
Thomas Harper.	Charles Miller.
Thomas Caulfield.	John Peareth.
William Greening.	Joseph Heath.
John Hunter.	John French, jun.
Thomas Parks.	George Eves.
William Bridgeman.	Samuel Roberts.

THE HALL-COMMITTEE

Consists of all past and present Grand Officers, and Mr. John Yeomans.

OFFICERS of the GRAND LODGE of ENGLAND, from its Revival, A. D. 1717, to the present Time.

GRAND MASTERS.

1717 Anthony Sayer, Esq.	1734 John Lindsey, E. of Crawford
1718 George Payne, Esq.	1735 T. Thynne, Ld Vis. Weymouth
1719 J. T. Desaguliers, LL. D. F. R. S.	1736 John Campbell, E. of Laudon
1720 George Payne, Esq.	1737 Edward Bligh, E. of Darnley
1721 John, D. of Montague	1738 H. Bridges, Marq. of Carnarvon
1722 Philip, D. of Wharton	1739 Robert Ld Raymond
1723 Francis Scott, E. of Dalkeith	1740 John Keith, E. of Kintore
1724 Cha. Lenox, D. of Richmond	1741 James Douglas, E. of Morton
1725 James Hamilton, Lord Paisley	1742-3 John Ld Vis. Dudley and Ward
1726 Wm. O'Brien, E. of Inchiquin	1744 Tho. Lyon, E. of Strathmore
1727 Henry Hare, Ld Coleraine	1745-46 James Ld Cranstoun
1728 James King, Ld Kingston	1747-51 William Byron, Ld Byron
1729-30 T. Howard, D. of Norfolk	1752-53 John Proby, Ld Carysfort
1731 T. Coke, Ld Lovel, afterwards	1754-56 James Bridges, Marq. of Car-
E. of Leicester.	narvon, afterw. D. of Chandos
1732 Ant. Brown, Ld Vis. Montague	1757-61 Sholto Douglas, Ld Aberdour
1733 James Lyon, E. of Strathmore	1762-63 Washing. Shirley, E. Ferrers
4	1764-66

(53)

1764-66 Cadwalladar, Ld Blaney   1777-82 G. Montague, D. of Manchester
1767-71 H. Somerset, D. of Beaufort   1783-90 His R. H. D. of Cumberland
1772-78 Robert Edward, Ld Petre   1791-96 His R. H. the Prince of Wales.

DEPUTY GRAND-MASTERS.

1721 John Beal, M. D.   1741 Martin Clare, A. M. F. R. S.
1722-23 J. Th. Defaguliers, LL.D. F. R. S.   1742-43 Sir Robert Lawley, Bart.
1724 Martin Folkes, Efq.   1744 William Vaughan, Efq.
1725 J. Th. Defaguliers, LL.D.   1745-46 Edw. Hody, M. D. F. R. S.
1726 William Cowper, Efq.   1747-51 Fotherley Baker, Efq.
1727 Alexander Choke, Efq.   1752-56 Tho. Manningham, M. D.
1728-30 Nath. Blackerby, Efq.   1757 61 John Revis, Efq.
1731-33 Thomas Batfon, Efq.   1762-67 Col. John Salter
1734 Sir Cecil Wray, Bart.   1768-74 Hon. Charles Dillon
1735-38 Jn. Ward, Efq. after. Ld Ward   1775 86 Rowland Holt, Efq.
1739-40 W. Græme, M. D. F. R. S.   1787-96 Sir Peter Parker. Bart.

GRAND WARDENS.

1717 Capt. John Elliot   1738 Lord George Graham
     Jacobus Lamball   Capt. Andrew Robinfon
1718 John Cordwell   1739 J. Harvey Thurfby, Efq.
     Thomas Morrice   Robert Foy, Efq.
1720 Thomas Hobby   1740 James Ruck, Efq.
     Richard Ware   W. Vaughan, Efq.
1721 Jofiah Villeneau   1741 W. Vaughan, Efq.
     Thomas Morrice   Benjamin Gafcoyne, Efq.
1722 Joshua Timfon   1742-43 E. Hody, M. D. F. R. S.
     J. Anderfon, A. M.   S. Berrington, Efq.
1723 Francis Sorrel, Efq.   1744 W. Græme, M. D. F. R. S.
     John Senex   Fotherly Baker, Efq.
1724 George Payne, Efq.   1745-46 Fotherly Baker, Efq.
     Francis Sorrel, Efq.   Thomas Smith, Efq.
1725 Col. D. Houghton   1747-51 Hon. Rob. Shirley
     Sir Thomas Pende.gaft, Bart.   Thomas Jeffreys, Efq.
1726 Alexander Choke, Efq.   1752 Hon. J. Carmichael
     W. Burdon, Efq.   Sir R. Wrottecy, Bart.
1727 Nathaniel Blackerby, Efq.   1753 Sir R. Wrottefley, Bart.
     Jofeph Highmore   Francis Blake Delaval, Efq.
1728 Sir J. Thornhill, Knt.   1754 Fleming Pingftan
     Mart. O'Conner   Arthur Beardmore
1729-30 Col. George Carpenter   1755 Hon. H. Townfend
     Thomas Batfon, Efq.   James Dickfon, Efq.
1731 George Douglas, M. D.   1756 James Nafh, Efq.
     James Chambers, Efq.   Bern. Joach. Boetefeur, Efq.
1732 George Rooks, Efq.   1757 William Chapman, Efq.
     James Moor-Smith, Efq.   Alexander Valdevelde, Efq.
1733 James Moor-Smith, Efq.   1758-59 J. Dickfon, Efq.
     Hon. John Ward   Thomas Singleton, Efq.
1734 Hon. John Ward   1760-61 G. Schombart, Efq.
     Sir Edward Manfell, Bart.   Charles Maffey, Efq.
1735 Sir Edward Manfell, Bart.   1762 Col. John Salter
     Mart. Clare, A. M. F. R. S.   Robert Groat, Efq.
1736-37 Sir Robert Lawley, Bart.   1763 Robert Groatj Efq.
     W. Græme, M. D. F. R. S.   Thomas Edmonds, Efq.

(54)

1764 Hon. Thomas Shirley
Thomas Alleyne, Efq.
1765 Richard Ripley, Efq.
Capt. Charles Tuffnal
1766 Peter Edwards, Efq.
Horatio Riple, Efq.
1767 Hon. Charles Dillon
Capt. A. Campbell
1768 Rowland Holt, Efq.
Henry Jaffray, Efq.
1769 Rowland Holt, Efq.
Charles Taylor, Efq.
1770 Rowland Holt, Efq.
Sir W. Williams Wynne, Bt.
1771 Sir W. Williams Wynne, Bt.
William Hodgfon, Efq.
1772 Sir Peter Parker, Knt.
William Atkinfon, Efq.
1773 John Croft, Efq.
J. Ferdinando Gillio, Efq.
1774 J Hatch, Efq. vice L. Wentworth
Henry Dagge, Efq.
1775 Thomas Parker, Efq.
John Hull, Efq.
1776 Col. John Deaken
George Harrifon, Efq.
1777 Capt. W. H. Pafcal
John Allen, Efq.
1778 Henry Dagge, Efq.
Charles Marfh, Efq.
1779 Right Hon. Ld Vifc, Tamworth
George Heffe, Efq.
1780 John Peach Hungerford, Efq.
Theoph. Tompfon Tutt, Efq.

1781 Sir John St. Aubyn, Bart.
James Galloway, Efq.
1782 Sir Herbert Mackworth, Bart.
Philip Champ. Crefpigny, Efq.
1783 Hon. Wafhington Shirley
Geo. William Carrington, Efq.
1784 Hon. William Ward
James Meyrick, Efq.
1785 James Hefeltine, Efq.
M. J Levy, Efq.
Sir Lionel Darell, Bart.
1786 Sir Nicholas Nugent, Bart.
Nathaniel Newnham, Efq.
1787 Rt Hon. Ld Macdonald
James Curtis, Efq.
1788 Thomas Fitzherbert, Efq.
George Atkinfon, M. D.
1789 George Shum, Efq.
William Tyler, Efq.
1790 Henry Crathorne, Efq.
James Neild, Efq.
1791 Thomas Swanton, Efq.
John Warre, Efq.
1792 Thomas Thompfon, Efq.
Benjamin Lancafter, Efq.
1793 John Dent, Efq.
Edmund Armftrong, Efq.
1794 John Dawes, Efq.
Arthur Tegart, Efq.
1795 John Meyrick, Efq.
George Corry, Efq.
1796 George Porter, Efq.
Richard Brettingham, Efq.

GRAND TREASURERS.

1730-37 Nath. Blackerby, Efq.
1738-52 John Jefse, Efq.
1753-65 George Clarke, Efq.

1766-85 Rowland Berkeley, Efq.
1786 96 James Hefeltine, Efq.

GRAND SECRETARIES.

1722-25 William Cowper, Efq.
1726 Edward Wilfon
1727-33 William head
1734-56 John Revis, Efq.
1757-67 Samuel Spencer

1768 Thomas French
1769-80 James Hefeltine, Efq.
1780-84 { James Hefeltine, Efq.
{ William White
1784 96 William White

GRAND SWORD-BEARERS.

1733-4 George Moody
1745 Thomas Slaughter
1746-55 Daniel Carne
1756-66 Mark Adfton
1767-68 Thomas Dyne
1769-71 William Smith
1772-75 John Drawas

1776-77 Francis Johnfton
1778 85 James Bottomley
1786 87 John Paiba
1788-90 James Bottomley
1791 Benjamin Lancafter
1791-96 Chev. B. Rufrini

GRAND

(55)

GRAND STEWARDS.

[Those marked P were Presidents; T. Treasurers; and S. Secretaries of their respective Boards.——The present Officers of the Stewards Lodge are specified in Italicks, and the Members of it are marked thus, *.]

1721 Josiah Villeneau	John Brydges, Esq.	John Ross, Esq.
1723 Henry Prude	Wyrriot Ormond, Ef.	Cha. Champion
Giles Clutterbuck	Arthur Moore, Esq.	Richard Sawle
John Shepherd	Vinal Taverner, Esq.	James Pringle
Capt. Benj. Hodges	ClaudCrespigny, Esq.	Francis Blythe
Edward Lambert	William Blunt, Esq.	1737 Sir Bouch. Wray, Bt.
Charles Kent	Col. John Pitt	Lew.Theobald, M.D.
1724 Capt. Sam. Tuffnell	Henry Tatam	Geo, Bothomly, Esq.
Giles Taylor	Thomas Griffith	Cha. Murray, Esq.
Capt. Nath. Smith	Solomon Mendez	Capt. John Lloyd
Rich. Crofts	1733 John Ward, Esq.	Capt. Cha. Scott.
Peter Paul Kemp	John Pollexfen, Esq.	Peter M'Cullock
North Stainer	H. Butler Pacy, Esq.	Tho. Jefferys
1725 John JamesHeidegger	John Read, Esq.	Peter Leige
1726-27 Edw. Lambert	Wm. Busby, Esq.	Tho. Boehm, Esq.
1728 John Revis, Esq.	Philip Barnes, Esq.	Benjamin Da Costa
Edwin Ward	J. Misaubin, M. D.	Nath. Adams
Samuel Stead	John Dwight	1738 Capt. An. Robinson
Theod. Cheriholm	Richard Baugh	Robert Foy, Esq.
William Benn	Thomas Shank	Ja. Colquhoun, Esq.
Gerard Hatley	James Cosens	Wm.Chapman, Esq.
William Wilson	Charles Robinson	Henry Higden, Esq.
William Tew	1734 Sir Ed. Mansell, Bt.	Harry Leigh, Esq.
William Hopkins	R.Rawlinson,LLD.FRS.	St. Beaumont, M.D.
Thomas Reason	C. Holzendorf, Esq.	Moses Mendez
Thomas Alford	Isaac Muere, Esq.	Geo. Monkman
H. Smart	Prescot Pepper, Esq.	Stephen Le Bas
1729-30 John Revis, Esq.	Christ. Nevile, Esq.	Christopher Taylor
Samuel Stead	Rich.Matthews, Esq.	Simon de Charmes
Edwin Ward	Fotherly Baker, Esq.	1739 Jn. Chichester, Esq.
William Wilson	Sam.Berrington, Esq.	Edward Masters
Thomas Reason	John Pitt, Esq.	Jos. Harris
William Tew	Wm. Verelst, Esq.	Rich. Robinson
——— Pread	H.Hutchinson, Esq.	Paul Hen. Robinson
——— Bardo, sen	1735 Sir R. Lawley, Bt.	Isaac Barret
——— Bardo, jun,	W.Græme,M D.F.R.S.	Nath. Old. a
Charles Hoare	Mart.Clare,A.M.F.R.S.	Alex. Pollock
William Serjeant	J. Theobald, M. D.	Tho. Adamson
James Chambers, Es.	M.Schomberg,M D.	Thomas Parry
1731 G. Douglas, M. D.	Cap.Ral.Fairwinter,	Geo. Armstrong
J. Chambers, Esq	Ch. Fleetwood, Esq.	Sam. Lowman
Tho. Moore, Esq.	Tho. Beech, Esq.	1740 Esquire Cary
John Atwood, Esq.	Robert Wright	Mansel Bransby
Tho. Durant, Esq.	Thomas Slaughter	W. Vaughan, Esq.
George Page	James Nash	John Fabe.
John Haines	William Hogarth	John Saint
William Milward	1736 E.Hody,M.D.F.R.S.	John Soudon
Roger Lacy	I.Schomberg, jun.M.D.	James Bernard
Charles Teinquand	J. Ruck, jun. Esq.	David Dumouchel
John Calcot	John Gouland	Bryan Dawson
John King	Benjamin Gascoyne	William Ruck
1732 George Rook, Esq.	Walter Weldon	Mich. Comburne
J. Moor Smyth, Esq.	John Jesse	George Mason

152

1741 Count. E. Fr. Taube
Daniel Carne
James Wallace
John Gordon
Peter Hamet
George Caton
William Salt
William Arnold
Lewis de Vaux
Edward Rudge
Richard Shergold
James Spranger
1742-3 Edward Trevor
Talbot Waterhouse
Ro. Bateman Wray
Ant. Benn
Stephen Rogers
Peter Le Maistre
John Trail, A. M.
Henry Liel, Esq.
Edm. Brydges
William Vol
Thomas Pownal
Jos. Lycett
1744 John Coggs
Tho. Clipperton
Tho. Leddiard, Esq.
Charles Dubuy
Luke Alder
Robert Mitchel
H. & Rev. O. Dawnay
Wm. Mountaine
Thomas Griffiths
Tho. Smith, Esq.
John Torr
Peter Gordon
1745-6 Francis Jackman
George Pile, M. D.
John Villeneau
Geo. Powlett, Esq.
James Whitworth
William Rogers
John Stone
James Bennet, Esq.
James Wilsford
Tho. Chaddocke
Robert Cheeke
Fleming Pinkstan
1747-51 Mat. Creyghton
John Feary
Peter Clerke
Rob. Shirley, Esq.
Robert Young
William Rogers
Jos. Lycett
John Spranger
T. Maningham, M. D.
Pheasant Hartley
George Clarke
Col. S. Berrington

1752 Hon. J. Carmichael
Sir R. Wrottesly, Bt.
Ber. Joac. Boetefeur
Robert Marcelius
George Steidell
Stephen Yonge
Richard Lane
Thomas Taylor
Charles Wade
John Jourdan
Jos. Brunett
George Forbes
1753 Peter Leigh, Esq.
John Price
Tho. Apreece, Esq.
H. Cap. W. Montague
F. Blake Delaval, Esq.
Cap. Edw Byre
James Shrudder
William Blett
Mark Adkton
Henry Smith
Buckle Bankin
Rich. Savage, Esq.
1754 Arthur Beardmore
James Dickson
Samuel Markham
Samuel Spencer
George Dumar
David Humphreys
Martin Capron
Hon. Cap. Ch. Proby
William Singleton
John Atkinson
Godfrey Springal
Thomas Douglas
1755 Hon. Ho. Townsend
Rev. John Entick
Rev. Martin Despres
James Shepheard
James Gifford
Albert Vandevelde
Christian Heineken
Caspar Schombart
Frederick Maurer
Thomas Singleton
William Townsend
Charles Pearce
1756 Thomas Haward
Charles Hoyle
Martin Klincke
William Andrews
Thomas Cobb
James Pollard
Henry Gunter
Th. Marriott Perkins
Mark Goodflesh
Joseph Axtel
Gabriel Risoliere
Charles Massey

1757 Humphrey Jackson
Richard Hill
Fred. Van Gehten
Paul R---thon
Joh. Young
Robert Lloyd
Kenrick Peck
John Darby
Langford Millington
Thomas Clegg
John Wildsmith
Adam Nuttall
1758-9 Adam Nuttall
Abraham Hatt
Jonathan Scott
Frederick Kohtd
Ralph Bates, Esq.
John Rowley
Philip Scriven
George Rudd
Capt. Chas Tuffnell
Thomas Williams
Obadiah Wright
James Whealey
1760
P.   William Smith
T.   Row. Berkeley, Esq.
S.   John Burrell
William Potler
Robert Harding
John Friday
George Restell
William Barbar
John Ask, Esq.
John Ramsay
Thomas Smith
Robert Jones
1762
Col. John Salter
Robert Groat
Robert Laurie
Henry Jaffray
Sir Rich. Glynn, Bt.
Stephen Day
William Chapman
Francis Bickerton
Thomas Dyne
------ Dun
John Benson
Bryant Troughton
1763
Joseph Power
Thomas Alleyne
Christian Poppe
Capt Moller
Richard Wright
Philip Cole
William Hodgson
Tho. Edmonds, sen.
Charley Churchman

(7)

George Carnaby	
Richard Hearne	
Hon. Tho. Harley	
1764	
Thomas Treflore	
John Nix	
James Alleyne	
Thomas Shirley, Esq.	
Edward Hoare	
Wm Ashburner	P.
Jonathan Mitchie	T.
John Collack	S.
James Burgess	
Thomas Edmonds	
Thomas Woolsey	
William Wray	
1765	
Ant. Keck, Esq.	
Richard Ripley, Esq.	
Ant. Ten Broeke	
John Forbes	
Peter Edwards	
Joshua Kitson	P.
Christ. Cutterel	T.
John Nix	S.
Joseph Dixon	
Rice Williams	
Horatio Ripley, Esq	
George Forbes	
1766	
—— Pye, Esq.	
Wm. Cuthbertson	
Robert James	
Pingth Blackwood	
Dr. St. John	
William Collins	P.
Ant. Daveyer	T.
Peter Laimillier	S.
Richard Ditkson	
Ant. Girardot, Esq.	
Geo. Paterson, Esq.	
John Mitchie, Esq.	
1767	
P. Capt. Ali Campbell	
T. Lieu. Col. Twisleton	
S. F. Twisleton, Esq.	
Charles Taylor, Esq.	
Thomas Brooke	
*James Hefeltine, Esq.	P.
Thomas French	T.
Hon. Charles Dillon	S.
Narhaniel Serjeant	
H. V. Oudermeulen	
Edw. Shepherd, Esq.	
Samuel Way, Esq.	
1768	
P. Rowl. Holt, Esq.	
T. Major John Deaken	
S. John Derwas	
Richard Rose Drew	

John Bowman	
John Richardson	P.
William Settree	T.
Jervis Critchley	S.
John Maddocks	
Francis Johnston	
James Leishman	
Peter Rancer	
1769	
Col. Ch. Rainsford	
******	
William Birch, Esq.	
Eph. Gotlieb Muller	
John Allen, Esq.	
William Paterson	P.
Thomas Settree	T.
Edward Knightley	S.
Thomas Lecon	
Peter Vestenburg	
Capt. P. Hardwicke	
John Anderson	
1770	
Sir W. W. Wynne, Bt.	
John Dobbins	
Stephen Freneau	
Hon. H. S. Conway	
William Eden, Esq.	
Peter Anf. Delius	P.
J. Farmer	T.
Joseph Binley	S.
John Wilson	
Henry Dagge, Esq.	
George Hayter	
J. W. Holwell, Esq.	
1771	
Sir T. Tancred, Bt	P.
W. Atkinson, Esq.	T.
George Gillio, Esq.	S.
Sir John Blois, Bt.	
Dominic Mead, Esq.	
Henry Chittick, Esq	P.
Thomas Brown, Esq.	T.
Alex. Moultre, Esq.	S.
John Brockbank	
Ja. Bottomley	
James Harrison	
Thomas Williamson	
1772	
Sir P. Parker, Bt.	P.
*J. Galloway, Esq.	T.
I. Ferd. Gillio, Esq.	S.
Theob. Burke, Esq.	
John Townson, Esq.	
Thomas Evance, Esq.	P.
Thomas Parker, Esq.	T.
John Shaw	S.
John Johnson	
Hon. Edm. Butler	
John Bailey, Esq.	
*Bart. Ruspini	

1773	
John Croft, Esq.	P.
James Nield, Esq.	T.
John Hull, Esq.	S.
Hon. Tho. Noel	
Robert Sparrow, Esq.	
William Harris, Esq.	
Naph. Franks, Esq.	
William Crozier	
John Ainslie	
John Hewitt	
Lowen Head	
Thomas Daw	
1774	
F. Minshull, Esq.	P.
Richard Barker, Esq.	T.
Peter Simond, Esq.	S.
John Hatch, Esq.	
Sir T. Fowke, Knt.	
Robert Butler, Esq.	
George Durant, Esq.	
Thomas Martin	
Richard Templar	
*Alexander Dew, S.	
James Mist	
Robert Brown Esq.	
1775	
Capt. C. Frederick	P.
T. Tomson Tutt, Esq.	T.
*William White	S.
Capt. A. Murray	
Capt. George Smith	
Thomas Lynch, Esq.	
Walter Smith, Esq.	
William Atkinson	
John Turner	
Cuthbert Potts	
Edmund Smith	
Alexander M'Kowl	
1776	
Capt. M. H. Pascal	P.
Char. Marsh, Esq.	T.
Geo. Harrison, Esq.	S.
Tho. Meggison, Esq.	
Rd. Troward, Esq.	
Fr. Sey. Cosby, Esq.	
Rd. Drake, Esq.	
James Crosby	
Edward Trelawney	
*John Bain	
John Ducket	
Aaron Bateman	
1777	
Ja. Worsley, Esq.	P.
R. Franco, Esq.	T.
*Rev. John Frith, S.W.	S.
George Hesse, Esq.	
John Cooper	
Dr. Isaac Sequeira	
Rich. Gamon, Esq.	

154

Dr. Reynolds — S.
Row. Dawk. Mansell
Edward Halfhide
*Adam Donford
John Mills
1778
P. Hon. Ld C. Montag.
T. Benjamin Lyon, Esq.
S. G. W. Carrington, Esq.
T. H. Broadhead, Esq.
Rt. Biggin, Esq.
Geo. Lempriere, Esq. — P.
Thomas Wright — T.
Jonathan White — S.
J. Richlardi
*J. Yeomans
William Omans
John Pilkington
1779
P. The Earl Ferrers
T. Joseph Newton, Esq.
S. James Pears.
Annesley Sheo
T. B. Handasyd
Fred. Abel, Esq.
George Grieve, Esq.
John Hempsted
Joseph Newnham
Jac. Torban
Rowland Minns
Andrew O'Brien
1780
P. Francis Franco, Esq.
T. C. Vanderstop, Esq.
S. Ol. Crom. Vile
Percival Pott, Esq.
*Sherborne Stuart, Esq.
J. P. Hungerford, Esq.
James Johnston
*Joseph Smith
*William Fry
John Serjeant
John Mettenius
*Wm. Collins, jun. Esf.
1781
P. M. I. Levy, Esq.
T. Peter Plank
S. *John Marshall
Henry Cotton
John Ratcliffe
Philip Crespigny, Esq.
John Kupky
William Fleming
George Hartman
Frederick Bach
William Hough
*Sir John St. Aubyn, Bt.
1782
P. Sir H. Mackworth, Bt.
T. Thomas Preston, Esq.

*Edward Hill
Samuel Benge
George Barclay
*James Carr — P.
*Fleming French — T.
B. Lancaster, Esq. — S.
William Mayne
John Paiba
*Robert Pington
*Benjamin Skutt, Sec.
1783
Hon. Wash. Shirley — P.
James Meyrick, Esq. — T.
William Faden — S.
William Tyler, Esq.
W. Mitch. Sale, Esq.
William Morse
Abr. Nunes
Thomas Settree, jun.
*James Rowley
*Simeon Pope
*Samuel Fulham
*William Miller
1784
Hon. Wm. Ward — P.
*Isaac Serra, Esq. — T.
John Tho. Cox, Esq. — S.
*Henry Crathorne, Esf.
Earnest Cramer
Redm. Simpson
*Stephen Clark, Tr.
Thomas Lambert
John Miller
James Fozard
John Harris, Esq.
Isaac Lindo
1785
*Sir N. Nugent, Bt. — P.
N. Newnham, Esq. — T.
* J. J. Pritchard — S.
Lionel Darell, Esq.
Arthur Onslow, Esq.
Capt. Christ. Parker — P.
*John Ungerland — T.
*James Massey — S.
*James Johnston
Dr. Steph. Freeman
Isaac Moron
*Thomas Patrick
1786
Rt Hon. Ld Macdonald — P.
Robert Ingram, Esq. — T.
*William Earle — S.
*Col. Tho. Swanton
Richard Baldwyn
*Wm. Fynmore, Esq. — P.
*John Pierce — T.
George Wright — S.
*R. Dennison
A. Garcia

*Thomas Hartley
*Thomas Pugh
1787
*Thomas Croft, Esq. — P.
*Col. W. D. Clephane — T.
S. W. Wadeson, Es. — S.
James Curtis, Esq.
Dr. T. S. Dupuis
John Lewis, Esq.
G. Errington, Esq.
*Alexander Dewar
*Robert Lambert
D. Aguilar
Geo. Blakiton
Benjamin Lloyd
1788
Tho. Fitzherbert, Es. — P.
William Shard, Esq. — T.
T. Calender — S.
George Atkinson
Duncan Campbell, Es.
Robert Ritherdon
James Howell
Charles Wren
*Thomas Barber
*William Daw, J.W.
*Ephraim France
*E. Jendun
1789
*George Shum, Esq. — P.
Edm. Armstrong, Es. — T.
John Byng — S.
R. Baddeley
J. Raincock, Esq.
*Robert Griffin
Sam. Vita Montefiore
*William Virgoe
*James Steers, Esq.
Tho. Thompson, Es.
M. Lascelles
*John Edwards
1790
John Warre, Esq.
Thomas Ingram, 2.
*Samuel Plaisted
R. Molesworth, Esq.
*John M'Donald
*R. W. Jennings, Esq.
Nicholas Lambert
*Joseph Nourse, Esq.
*Francis Virgoe
John Read, Esq.
*J. I. Cossart
*James Robinson
1791
*John Dent, Esq. — P.
*James Sayer — T.
*W. C. Clarkson — S.
*R. Brettingham
*R. W. Bridgman, Esq.

(59)

*William Marsh
*James Whittle
*Edward Fitch
*William Pitter
Count Duroure
*S. Clanfield
*John Meyrick, Esq.
1792
P. *Rich. Harborne, Es.
T. *E. D. Batson, Esq.
S. *James Bliss
Geo. Fred. Parry, Es.
Will.Hen.Pigou, Es.
*Fran. L. Morgan
*David Bucklee
*Robert Salmon
Thomas Hyde
*William Martin
*Robert Best
*James Bradshaw, Es.
1793
P. *G.Corry,Esq.P.M.
T. *Arthur Tegart, Esq.
S. *John Dickinson
*Charles Clarke
*John Dawes, Esq.
*John Whitfield
*William Tremain
*Don. Macdonald

*R.L.Fladgate, P.M.
Col. William Draper
*David Gwynne   P.
*Thomas King   T.
1794   S.
*Hon.T.J.Twisleton
*Nath. Gostling, Esq.
*Rd Woodward, Esq.
*The Earl of Pomfret
*Sir W. J. James, Bt.
*ThomasFellowes,Es.
*RichardGriffiths, Es.
*John Rush, Esq.
*Cha. Carpenter, Esq.
*John Johnstone, Esq.
*JosephKnowles, Esq.
*Robert Randoll, Esq.
1795
*S. S. Baxter, Esq.   P.
*George Bolton, Esq.   T.
*Thomas Hill, Esq.   S.
*Arthur Gower, Esq.
*William Ayres
*John Godwin
*William Newton
*John Steward
*George Porter, Esq.
*Mat. Wilson, Esq.
*William Gill, Esq.

*W. Blackstone, Esq.
1796
*Sir John Eamer
*L. R. Mackintosh
*James Duberley
*William Veel
*Jos. Dennison
*Robert Sutton
*Thomas Harper
*Thomas Caulfield
*W. Greening
*John Hunter
*Thomas Parkes
*W. Bridgeman
*The following were present-
ed as G. S. for 1797.*
*R. H. Bradshaw
*Bailey Heath
*John Bullock
*Charles Turner
*Robert Harper
*T. A. Losley
*Charles Millett
John Peareth
*Joseph Heath
*John French, jun.
*George Eves
*Samuel Roberts

LIST of SUBSCRIBERS to the HALL-LOAN, agreeable to a Resolution of the GRAND LODGE, on 21st June, 1779.

His R. H. the D. of Cumberland, P. G. M.

Duke of Manchester, P. G. M.	Earl Ferrers, P. S. G. W.
Lord Petre, P. G. M.	Earl of Antrim
Earl of Effingham, P. A. G. M.	Earl Ferrers, P. S. G. W.
Sir Peter Parker, Bt. D. G. M.	G. William Carrington, Esq.
Rowland Holt, Esq. P. D. G. M.	James Meyrick, Esq.
J. Heseltine, Esq. P. S. G. W. and G. T.	Sir Lionel Darell, Bart.
Thomas Sandby, Esq. G. A.	Nath. Newnham, Esq.
John Croft, Esq.	James Nield, Esq.
Thomas Parker, Esq.	Benj. Lancaster, Esq.
Henry Dagge, Esq.	Rowland Berkeley, Esq. P. G. T.
Sir John St. Aubyn, Bt.	Mr. James Bottomley, P. G. S. B.
Sir Herbert Mackworth, Bt.	Henry Harford, Esq.
Hon. William Ward	Chev. Bartholomew Ruspini
M. I. Levy, Esq.	Mr. William Rigge
Sir Nic. Nugent, Bart.	Mr. Peter Plank
Thomas Dunckerley, Esq.	John Beardsworth, Esq.
William Hodgson, Esq.	William Pickett, Esq.
William Atkinson, Esq.	Mr. John Pilkington
John Hull, Esq.	Mr. John Hodges
George Harrison, Esq.	Benjamin Lyon, Esq.
John Allen, Esq.	Mr. Joseph Procter
Charles Marsh, Esq.	Percival Pott, junior, Esq.
George Hesse, Esq.	Mr. Edward Hill
T. Tompson Tutt, Esq.	John Philip Merckle, Esq.
James Galloway, Esq.	Francis Franco, Esq.
P. Champion Crespigny, Esq.	Sir Stephen Lushington, Bart.

I   Sir

(60)

	L O D G E S.
Sir Barnard Turner, Knt,	
William Shard, Esq.	The Grand Stewards' Lodge
Mr. William Fry	2 Somerset-house L. FreemasonsTav.
John Harris, Esq.	3 L. of Friendship, Thatched-h. Tav.
James Barbut, Esq.	12 L. of Emulation, Paul's-head Tav.
Jacob Appleby, Esq.	19 Castle-l. of Harmony, Doct. Comm.
Mr. Richard Cox	23 St. Alban's Lodge, Dover-street
Mr. Jessintour Rozea	29 Britannic Lodge, Pall-mall
Mr. Henry Strickland	39 Royal Cumberland Lodge, Bath
Mr. Alexander M'Kowl	46 Fountain court, Strand
Mr. Robert Cook	86 Prince George, Plymouth
Mr. George Donadieu	95 L. of Love and Honour, Falmouth
Mr. William Barker	114 Rose & Crown, Crown-st. Westm.
Mr. John Piper	146 Shakespeare, Covent-garden
Robert Ingram, Esq.	162 London Lodge, Ludgate-street
Robert Butler, Esq.	211 Caledonian Lodge, Gracechurch-st.
Redmond Simpson, Esq.	216 Tuscan Lodge, Holborn
Christopher Parker, Esq.	218 Gothic L. Crown, Tufton-street
Isaac Serra, Esq.	238 George and Crown, Wakefield
Thomas West, Esq.	294 L. of Virtue, White Lion, Bath
The Rev. Edmund Gardener	358 Lodge of Jehosaphat, Bristol
Cha. Phillott, Esq.	369 Lodge of Liberty and Sincerity,
Wm. Street, Esq.	Bridgewater
Milbourn West, Esq.	403 L. of Honour, Broad-way, Westm.
Dr. Tho. Sanders Dupuis	407 L. of Nine Muses, St. James's-str.
Thomas Hartley, Esq.	411 Gnoll Lodge, Neath
H. Spirling, Esq.	462 Royal Gloucester L. Bell, Glouc.
Sam. Tysson, Esq.	474 Harmonic Lodge, Hampton-court
Hugh Dixon, Esq.	

REMARKABLE OCCURRENCES IN MASONRY.

ST. Alban formed the first Grand Lodge in Britain A. D. 287	Book of Constitutions first published — 1723
King Athelstan granted a Charter to Free-masons — 926	Grand Secretary first established 1723
Prince Edwin formed a Grand Lodge at York — 926	Grand Treasurer appointed 1724
Edwin the IIId. revised the Constitutions — 1358	A general Fund proposed for distressed Masons — 1724
Masons' Assemblies prohibited by Parliament — 1425	Committee of Charity established 1725
Henry VI. initiated — 1450	Provincial Grand Masters first appointed — 1726
Grand Masters of the Knights of Malta, Patrons of Masonry 1500	Twelve Grand Stewards first appointed — 1728
Inigo Jones constituted several Lodges — 1607	Lord Kingston gave valuable Presents to the Grand Lodge 1729
Earl of St. Alban regulated the Lodges — 1637	Duke of Norfolk, ditto 1731
St. Paul's begun by Freemasons 1657	The Emperor of Germany initiated 1735
William the IIId privately initiated 1690	Grand Stewards Lodge first established 1735
St.Paul's completed by Freemason. 1713	Frederic Prince of Wales initiated 1737
Grand Lodge revived, Anthony Sayer, Esq. G. M. — 1717	Anderson's Edition of the Constitution-Book published 1738
Several Noblemen initiated 1719	Grand Hall built at Antigua 1744
Valuable MSS burnt by scrupulous Brethren. — 1720	Public Processions on Feast Days discontinued — 1747
Office of Deputy Grand Master revived — 1720	Grand Certificates first issued 1755
	Fourteen Persons expelled for Irregularity — 1757

Entick's

4

157

(61)

Entick's Edition of the Conftitution Book publifhed —	1758	Freemafons Calendar publifhed by Authority of the Grand Lodge	1777
Fifty Pounds diftributed in Charity abroad — —	1760	Anniverfary of Dedication ordered to be kept —	1777
Several Perfons expelled for Irregularities —	1762	Several Mafons imprifoned at Naples —	1777
His Royal Highnefs the Duke of Gloucefter initiated	1766	Fees of conftituting Lodges and making Mafons raifed	1777
A new Edition of Conftitutions ordered — —	1767	Several Princes of Germany formed a Lodge —	1777
Henry Frederic Duke of Cumberland initiated —	1767	His Royal Highnefs the Duke of Cumberland elected G. M.	1782
One Hundred Pounds fent to Barbadoes for Sufferers by Fire	1768	Noorthouck's Edition of the Book of Conftitutions printed	1784
Regiftering-Regulations commenced 29 October —	1768	His Royal Highnefs the Prince of Wales initiated —	1787
Plan of a Hall for the Grand Lodge approved —	1769	His Royal Highnefs Prince William Henry initiated	1787
Elegant Hall built by the Freemafons at Barbadoes	1772	His Royal Highnefs the Duke of York initiated —	1787
Hall-Committee appointed by the Grand Lodge	1773	Increafed Regiftering-Regulation on Town Lodges commenced 5 May —	1788
Alliance formed with the Grand Lodge of Germany —	1773	Freemafons' Tavern rebuilt	1788
King of Pruffia incorporated the Society in Pruffia —	1774	Royal Cumberland Freemafon School inftituted	1788
Ground purchafed for a Hall in London — —	1774	His Royal Highnefs Prince Edward initiated —	1790
Firft Stone of Freemafon's Hall laid — —	1775	His Royal Highnefs the Duke of Cumberland, G. M. died	1790
Five Thoufand Pounds raifed by a Tontine towards building ditto	1775	His Royal Highnefs the Prince of Wales elected G. M.	1790
Office of Grand Chaplain revived	1775	His Royal Highnefs Prince William of Gloucefter initiated	1795
Appendix to Books of Conftitutions publifhed —	1776	His Royal Highnefs Prince Erneft Auguftus initiated	1796
Freemafons Hall dedicated	1776		
Office of Grand Architect eftablifhed —	1776		

General Meetings of the Society in 1796.

Committee of Charity — — —	Friday,	February	5.
Quarterly Communication — —	Wednefday,	Ditto	8.
Committee of Charity — — —	Friday,	April	7.
Quarterly Communication — —	Wednefday,	Ditto	12.
Grand Feaft — — —	Wednefday,	May	10.
Country Feaft — — —	Wednefday,	July	5.
Committee of Charity — — —	Friday,	Auguft	4.
Ditto — — —	Friday,	Nov.	17.
Quarterly Communication — —	Wednefday,	Ditto	22.

LODGES *erafed* for not conforming to the Laws of the Society, or *difcontinued* on being united to other Lodges, fince the Alteration of the Numbers in 1792.

1794.	
49 Lodge of St. George de l'Obfervance, Covent garden	294 St. John's Lodge, Newmarket
90 Sea-Captains Lodge, Leadenhall-ftreet	327 St. Peter's Lodge, Mount-ftreet, *united* to Lodge of Prudence, No. 69, now the Lodge of Prudence and Peter

I 2

380 Loge

158

(62)

380 Loge d'Ega'ité, *united* to the ancient French Lodge, No. 110, now Loge d's Amis Réunis
399 At Futty-Ghur, Bengal
409 Royal Navy Lodge, Gosport
431 Pythagorean Lodge, Richmond, Surrey
467 Harodim Lodge, *united* to No. 1, the Lodge of Antiquity

1795.
307 St. Michael's, at Schwerin, in Mecklenburg

174 St. Nicolas's Lodge, Harwich
311 Helvetic - Union Lodge, Leaden-hall-street

1796.
207 Star Lodge, Chester
336 Impregnable Lodge, Sandwich
350 Lodge of Rural Friendship, *united* to No. 330, Lodge of the Nine Muses
393 St. Margaret's Lodge, Dartmouth-street, Westminster

LIST of LODGES, with their Numbers, as altered by Order of the Grand Lodge, April 18, 1792.

The GRAND STEWARDS' LODGE, (*constituted* 1735,) Freemasons' Tavern, 3d Wed. from Oct. to May. Public Nights, 3d Wed. in March and Dec.

Time immemorial.

1 Lodge of Antiquity, Freemasons' Tavern. Great Queen-str. (formerly the Goose and Gridiron, St. Paul's Church-yard) 4th Wednesday in Winter
2 Somerset-house Lodge, Freemasons' Tavern, 2d and 4th Mondays
1721
3 Lodge of Friendship, Thatched-house Tavern, St. James's-street
4 British Lodge, Nag's Head, Carnaby-square, 1st and 3d Tues.
5 Westminster and Key-stone Lodge, Horn Tav. Palace-yard, 1st Mond.
1722.
6 Lodge of Fortitude, King's Arms Tavern, Old Compton-street, 1st and 3d Wed.
7 Lodge of St. Mary-le-bonne, Cavendish-square Coffee-house, 3d M.
8 Ionic Lodge, King's Arms, Brook-str. Grosvenor sq. 3d Wed.
9 Dundee-arms Lodge, their private Room, Red-lion-st. Wapping, 2d and 4th Th.
1723.
10 *Kentish Lodge of Antiquity, Sun Tav. Chatham, 1st and 3d M.*
11 *King's Arms, Wandsworth, Surrey*
12 Lodge of Emulation, Paul's-head Tav. Cateaton-st. 3d M.
13 *Fraternal Lodge, Greyhound Tav. Stockwell-st. Greenwich, 4th Tu.*
14 Globe Lodge, White Hart Tav. Holborn, 1st Th.
15 Jacob's Ladder, Bolt and Tun, Silver-st. Fleet-st.
1724
16 *White Swan, St. Peter's, Norwich, 1st Wed.*

17 *Lodge of Antiquity, Three Tuns, Portsmouth*
18 Castle Lodge of Harmony, Horn, Doctors Com. 1st and 3d M. Win. 1st M. Sum.
19 *Lodge of Philanthropy, Black Lion, Stockton-upon-Tees, Durham, 1st and 3d Frid.*
1725.
20 Lodge of Cordiality, Chancery Coffee-house, Southampton-buildings, Chancery-l. 4th M.
21 Old King's-arms Lodge, Freemasons' Tav. 1st Th. from Oct. to May, inclusive
1727.
22 St. Alban's Lodge, Thomas's Tav. Dover-st. Piccadilly, 1st M.
1728.
23 Lodge of Attention, Freemasons' Tav. 2d and 4th Th.
1729.
24 St. John's Lodge, at Gibraltar, 1st Tu.
1730.
25 Castle Lodge, White Swan, Mansfel-st. Goodman's Fields, 1st Th.
26 The Corner-stone Lodge, Thatched-house Tav. St. James's-st. 2d M.
27 Britannic Lodge, Star and Garter, Pall-mall
28 *Well-disposed Lodge, at the Cock, Waltham Abbey, 1st Sat.*
29 Lodge of Fortitude, Crown and Thistle, East Smithfield, 2d W.
1731.
30 Sociable Lodge, Horn Tav. Doctor's Commons, 4th M.
31 *Medina L. Vire, West Cowes, S. 1st & 3d Th. W. Th. near full Moon*
32 King's Arms, Marybone-st. Piccadilly, 2d and 4th Tu.
33 *Anchor and Hope, Bolton-le-Moor, Lancashire, Th. on or after full Moon*
34 *Sarum Lodge, a private Room, George-court, High-st. Salisbury, 1st and 3d W.*

35 St.

(63)

35 *St. John's Lodge, Half-moon, Fore-st. Exeter, 2d and laſt F.*
1733.
36 *Royal Cumberland Lodge, Bear Inn, Bath, 1ſt and 3d F.*
37 *Lodge of Relief, Swan, Bury, Lancaſhire, next Th. to every full M.*
38 St. *Paul's Lodge, Shakeſpear Tav. Birmingham, 1ſt and 3d F.*
39 Royal Exchange, Boſton in New England, 2d and 4th Sat.
40 Valenciennes, French Flanders, 2d and 4th Sat.
1734.
41 Strong Man, Eaſt Smithfield, late the Ship, at the Hermitage, 1ſt Th.
1735.
42 *Swan, Wolverhampton, 1ſt & 3dTh.*
43 Union L. of Freedom and Eaſe, Surrey Tav. Surrey-ſt. Strand, 2d Tu.
44 *Lodge of Induſtry, Roſe and Crown, Swalwell, Durham, 1ſt M. and 3d S.*
45 Solomon's Lodge, Charles-town, South Carolina, 1ſt and 3d Th.
46 Solomon's Lodge, No. 1, Savannah, in Georgia, 1ſt and 3d Th.
47 *Angel, Colcheſter, 2d and 4th Tu.*
1736.
8 *King's Head, Norwich, laſt Th.*
50 Conſtitutional Lodge, Old Crown & Cuſhion, Lambeth-Marſh, 4th M.
51 *Howard Lodge of Brotherly Love, Crown, Arundel, Suſſex, 1ſt and 3d M.*
1737.
52 Parham L. Parham, in Antigua
53 City Lodge, Ship Tav. Leadenhall-ſt. 2d and 4th Th.
54 Lodge of Felicity, Queen's Arms Tav. St. James's ſt. 2d W.
55 Vacation Lodge, Star and Garter, Paddington, 4th W.
56 *Lodge of Affability, Caſtle Inn, New Brentford, 1ſt and 3d W.*
1738.
57 Royal Naval L. private Room, near Red-lion-ſt. Wapping, 1ſt & 3d W.
58 *Royal Cheſter Lodge, Feathers Inn, Bridge-ſt. Cheſter*
59 Baker's Lodge, St. John's, Antigua
60 Lodge of Peace and Harmony, Swan Tav. Fiſh-ſtreet-hill, 4th Th.
61 *Union Croſs, Halifax, Yorkſhire, 2d and 4th W.*
62 The Great Lodge, St. John's, Antigua, 2d and 4th W.
63 *Lodge of Fortitude, White Horſe, Hanging Ditch, Mancheſter, 2d M.*
1739.
64 Mother Lodge, at Kingſton, Jamaica, No. 1, 1ſt and 3d Sat.
65 Mother Lodge, Scotch Arms, at St. Chriſtopher's, Baſſeterre, 1ſt Th

66 Lodge of Sincerity, Joiners and Feltmakers Arms, Joiner-ſt. Southwark, 4th W.
67 Lodge of Peace and Plenty, Redlion, Horſlydown Lane, 2d Th. Maſter's Lodge, 5th Th.
68 Grenadiers' Lodge, Kings Arms, Brook ſt. Groſvenor-ſq. 2d W.
1740.
69 Lodge of Prudence and Peter, Bell, Upper Mount-ſt. 4th Th. Maſter's L. 5th Th.
70 Star in the Eaſt, at Calcutta, 1ſt Lodge of Bengal
71 St. Michael's Lodge, in Barbadoes
1742.
72 Lodge of Unity, Thiſtle and Crown, Suſſolk-ſt. Haymarket, 1ſt Th.
73 Old Road, St. Chriſtopher's
74 The Union, Franckfort, in Germany, 2d and 4th Th.
1743.
75 Prince George Lodge, George-town, Winyaw, South Carolina
1747.
76 Bear, Yarmouth, Norfolk
77 Lodge at St. Euſtatius
1748.
78 Angel, Norwich, 3d Tu.
79 *Prince George Lodge, Plymouth, 1ſt and 3d*
80 *Caſtle and Lion, St. Peter's Mancroſt, Norwich, 2d M.*
81 Second Lodge, Boſton, N. England, Br. Coffee h. King-ſt. 3d W.
82 No. 1. Halifax, in Nova Scotia
1750.
83 Marblehead Lodge, in Maſſachuſets. tay, New England
84 St. Chriſtopher's, at Sandy Point
85 Newhaven Lodge, in Connecticut, New England
1751.
86 *Unicorn, St. Mary's, Norwich, 2d and 4th W.*
87 *Lodge of Love and Honour, Royal Standard, Falmouth, 2d & laſt Th.*
88 Three Tuns, Great Yarmouth, Norfolt, laſt W.
89 *L. of Freedom, Pope's Head, Weſt-ſt. Graveſend, 1ſt and 3d Th.*
1752.
91 St. John's Lodge, Bridge-town, Barbadoes, 4th M.
92 George Lodge, Roſe and Crown, Downing-ſt. Weſtminſter, 3d Tu.
93 The Stewards Lodge, at Freemaſons' Hall, Madras, (revived 1786)
94 St. Peter's Lodge, Barbadoes, 1ſt and 3d S.
1753.
95 Old Cumberland Lodge, Red lion, Old

160

(64)

Old Cavendish-ft. Oxford ft. 2d Tu.

96 Foundation Lodge, Freemafons' Tav. Great Queen-ft. 2d W.

97 United Lodge of Prudence, Horfe Grenadier, near North Audley ft. Oxford-ft. 1ft Th.

98 Lily Tav. Guernfey

99 *Faithful Lodge, Vauxhall-Gardens, Norwich, 1ft and 3d W.*

100 Evangelifts' Lodge, at Montferratt

101 *Legs of Man, at Prefcot, Lancafhire, W. next before the full Moon*

102 Royal Exchange, Norfolk, in Virginia, 1ft Th.

1754.

103 *Druids' Lodge of Love and Liberality, London Inn, Redruth, Cornwall, 1ft and 3d Tu.*

104 Rofe and Crown, Crown-ft. Weftminfter, 2d Tu.

105 *Caftle and Lion, St. Peter's Mancroft, Norwich, 1ft and 3d M.*

106 *Scientific Lodge, Eagle and Child, Cambridge, 2d M.*

108 *St. James's Lodge, Crown Inn, Uxbridge, Middlefex, Th. neareft full Moon*

109 No. 2, at St. Fuftatius

110 Loge des Amis Réunis, Lewis's Coffee-h. Air-1. Piccadilly, 3d M.

111 *Lodge of Unanimity, Bull's Head, Manchefter, 1ft and 3d Tu.*

1755.

112 In the 8th or King's own Regiment of Foot, 1ft and 3d Tu.

113 Gloucefter Lodge, Rofe Tavern, Rofe alley, Bifhopfgate-ft. 3d W.

114 Lodge at Wilmington, on Cape-Fear River, North Carolina

115 Sea Captains' Lodge, Freemafons' T. St. Tho. Build. Liverpool, *every other Th.*

116 Union Lodge, Charles-town, South Carolina, 2d and 4th Th.

117 Lodge of Regulairty, Thatched h, Tav. St. James's-ft. 4th W.

118 Lodge of Freedom and Eafe, Three Jolly Butchers, Old-ftreet-road, 4th V.

119 Swan, at York-town, in Virginia, 1ft and 3d W.

120 *Wounded Hart, Norwich, 2d and 4th Tu.*

121 *Phœnix Lodge, Sunderland, Durham, 1ft & 3d W. Gen. 1ft W. Maft.*

122 Grand Lodge Frederick, at Hanover

123 *Loyal British Lodge, Red Tav. Eaft-Gate-ft. Chefter, 1ft M.*

1756.

124 St. David's Lodge, King's Arms Coffee-houfe, Brook-ft. 4th F.

125 A Mafters' Lodge, at Charlestown, South Carolina, 2d & 4th Th.

126 Port-Royal Lodge, Carolina, every other Wed.

127 Lodge of St. George, Ifland St. au Croix, in the Weft-Indies

128 Burlington Lodge, Coach and Horfes, Burlington-ft. 3d Th.

1757.

129 *Sea Captains' Lodge, King's Head, High-ft. Sunderland, 2d & 4th Th.*

130 Providence Lodge, in Rhode Ifland

131 Shakefpear, Covent-garden, 3d Th.

132 St. Mary's Lodge, St. Mary's Ifland, Jamaica

133 *Lodge of Friendfhip, White Horfe Tav. Norwich, 2d W.*

134 Lodge of Cordiality, Golden-crofs, Charing-crofs, 1ft W.

135 St. John's Lodge, Anne-ft. New York, No. 2, 2d and 4th W.

1758.

136 *King's Head, Coltifhal, Norfolk, W. near and before fall Moon*

137 *Lodge of Unity, King's Arms, Plymouth, 2d and 4th M. and 1ft Tu. Maft. L.*

138 *Beaufort Lodge, Cornifh-mount, on the Quay, Briftol, 1ft and 3d Tu.*

139 Lodge at Bombay, in the Eaft-Ind.

1759.

140 *Marine Lodge of Fortitude, Half-moon, Pembroke-ft. Plymouth-dock, 1ft and 3d Tu.*

141 *The Sun, at Newton-Abbot, Devonfhire, 2d Tu.*

1760.

142 London Lodge, London Coffee-h. Ludgate-hill, 1ft and 3d Tu.

1761.

143 Lodge of Induftry and Perfeverance, at Calcutta, 2d Lodge of Bengal

144 *Reftoration Lodge, private Room, at Prieft-gate, Darlington, laft Sa.*

145 Union Lodge, at Crow-lane, in Bermuda, 1ft W.

1762.

146 *St. George's Lodge, Globe Inn, Exeter, 2d and 4th Th.*

147 *British Union Lodge, Golden-lion, Ipfwich, Suffolk, 1ft Tu.*

148 Royal Frederic, at Rotterdam

149 *Royal Lancafhire Lodge, at the Hole in the Wall, Colne, in Lancafhire, 1ft Th.*

150 *St. Alban's Lodge, Shakefpear Tavern, Birmingham, 1ft & 3d Tu.*

151 Merchants' Lodge,

152 St. Andrew's Lodge, } at Quebec

153 St. Patrick's Lodge,

154 St. Peter's Lodge at Montreal

155 Select Lodge,

156 In the 52d Regiment } at Quebec of Foot,

157 Royal

(65)

157 *Royal Navy Lodge, Three-kings Inn, Deal, 1st M.*
158 *Lodge of Friendship, Crown, Lynn-Regis, Norfolk, 3d F.*
159 *Lodge of Inhabitants, at Gibraltar*
160 *Palladian Lodge, Bowling-Green, Hereford, 1st Tu.*
161 Door to Eternity, at Heldesham, in Germany
1763.
162 *Union Lodge, White-lion, Notting-ham, 3d Tu.*
163 St. Mark's Lodge, South Carolina
164 Lodge of Regularity, St. John's Hall, Black River, Musquito Shore, 1st and 3d Tu.
165 *Old Black Bull, at Richmond, in Yorkshire, 1st M.*
166 *Marquis of Granby Lodge, private Room, Old Elvit, Durham, 1st Tu.*
167 *L. of Amity, St. George's Quay, Bay of Honduras, 1st and 3d Tu.*
168 *Thorn, at Burnley, in Lancashire, Sat. nearest full Moon*
169 Union Lodge, Angel and Crown, Crispin-st. Spitalfields, 3d Th.
170 *Royal Mecklenburg Lodge, Green Dragon, Croydon, Surrey, 1st and 3d Tu.*
1764.
171 Royal Lodge, Thatched-h. Tav. St. James's-st. 1st F.
172 La Sagesse, St. Andrew, at the Grenadoes
173 *White-lion, at Kendal, in West-morland, 1st W.*
175 *White Hart, Ringwood, Hants*
176 *Lodge of Harmony, Red-lion, Feversham, 2d and 4th W.*
177 *Salutation, Topsham, Devonshire, 2d and 4th W.*
178 Lodge of Constitutional Attachment, Mitre, Tooley-st. 1st Th.
179 *Philharmonic L. at the Red-lion Inn, Isle of Ely, Cambridgesh. 1st M.*
180 Caledonian L. Guildhall Coffee-h. King-st. Cheapside, 1st M.
181 *Lodge of Perpetual Friendship, Lamb Inn, Bridgewater, Somer-set, 1st and 3d M.*
1765.
182 Lodge of St. John Evan. Two Blue Posts, Charlotte-st. Russel-p. Rathbone-p. 2d W.
183 British Social Lodge, White Bear, Old street-sq. 3d Tu.
184 Tuscan Lodge, King's Head Tav. Holborn, 3d Th.
185 Operative Masons, Cannon, Port-land-road, Marybone, 1st Tu. Mast. L. 5th Tu.
186 Gothick Lodge, Foot-guards Sut-tling-h. Whitehall, 4th M.

187 *Old Antelope Inn, Pool, in Dorset-shire, 1st and 3d W.*
188 Corinthian Lodge, Tiger, Wells-st. Oxford-st. 3d M.
189 *Tontine, Sheffield, in Yorkshire, 2d Frid.*
190 At Aloft, in Flanders
191 *St. George's Lodge, at the Castle, Lewisham, Kent, 1st M.*
192 *Black Horse, Tombland, Norwich, last F.*
193 *R. Edwin Lodge, Angel, Bury St. Edmunds, M. on or preceding full Moon*
194 *St. Luke's Lodge, Don Saltero's Coffee-h. Chelsea, 1st Tu.*
195 Lodge at Joppa, in Baltimore County, in Maryland
196 *L. of Perfect Friendship, White Hart Inn and Tav. Bath, 2d & 4th Tu.*
197 At St. Hilary, in Jersey
198 *Swan, at Warrington, in Lanca-shire, last M.*
199 Lodge of Perfect Unanimity, at Madras, No. 1, Coast of Coro-mandel (revived 1786)
200 Lodge, No. 1, Bencoolen
201 Tortola & Beef Island, 1st & 3d W.
1766.
202 *Lodge of Unanimity, Black Bull Inn, Wakefield, Yorkshire*
203 King's Arms Punch-house, Shad Thames, 1st M.
204 English Lodge, at Bourdeaux, (have met since the Year 1732)
205 Bedford Lodge, Freemasons' Tav. Great Queen-st. 1st W.
206 *Patriotic Lodge, Greyhound, Croydon, Surrey, Th. after every full Moon*
208 *St. Nicholas' Lodge, White Hart, Newcastle-upon-Tyne*
209 *Sion Lodge, private Room, North Shields, Northumberland, 2d Tu.*
210 *Lodge of True Friendship, Seven Stars, Bromley, Middlesex, 3d Tu.*
1767.
211 Angel, Upper Ground, Christ-church, Southwark, 3d Tu.
212 *Lodge of Integrity, Bull's Head Inn, Manchester, 1st M.*
213 *Union Lodge, Rising Sun, Castle Ditch, Bristol*
214 At Grenoble, in France
215 Lodge of Morality, King's Head, Old Compton-st. Soho, 2d Th.
216 Three Lions, Marborough, in Hessia
217 Lodge of Honour and Generosity, King's Head Tav Holborn, 1st Th.
218 Lodge of Union, Three Jolly Hat-ters, Bermondsey st. 3d W.
219 Royal York of Friendship, at Ber-lin, Middle Mark of Brandenburg
220 British

(66)

220 British Union, Rotterdam
221 St. John's Lodge, Flask Tavern, Hampstead, 1st Th.
222 Three Pillars, Rotterdam
223 Royal White Hart L. Halifax, North Carolina
224 Lodge of Amity, White Horse, Preston, Lancashire, 1st and 3d Th. Win. 1st Th. Sum.
225 Lodge of Amity, private Room, Canton, in China
226 All Souls Lodge, Tiverton, in Devonshire
227 L. Friendship, Angel, Illford, Essex, M. nearest full Moon, Mich. to Lady Day
1768.
228 Lodge of Concord, White-lion, High-st. Bloomsbury, 3d Tu.
229 Mona Lodge, King's Head, at Holyhead, Anglesea, N. Wales, every 3d F.
230 La Victoire, City of Rotterdam, in Holland
231 L. Sincerity. Gregorian's Arms, near Jamaica-row, Bermondsey, 2d Tu.
232 Caveac Lodge, Angel, Hammersmith, 1st Tu.
233 In the 24th Regiment of Foot
234 Constant Union, the City of Ghent, in Flanders
235 Godolphin Lodge, St. Mary's Island, Scilly
236 Manchester Lodge, Nott's Coffee-h. Butcher-row, Temple-bar, 1st W.
237 Lodge of Perfect Union, in his Sicilian Majesty's Reg. of Foot, Naples
238 L'Espérance, Thatched-h. Tav. St. James's-st. 1st M.
239 Qu. Charlotte's Lodge, Ashley's Punch-house, Ludgate-hill, 2d Th.
1769.
240 Sun Lodge, in the City of Flushing, in the Province of Zealand
241 Lodge of Hope, Crown, Stourbridge, Worcestershire
242 Lodge of Unity, K. Henry's Head, Red-lion-st. Whitechapel, 4th M.
243 Royal George L. at Newton Abbot
244 Beaufort Lodge, at Swansea
245 Well-chosen Lodge, at Naples
246 Lodge of Virtue, White-lion, Market-place, Bath, 1st & 3d M.
247 Inflexible Lodge, White Hart, Mitcham, Surrey. W. nearest full M.
248 Lodge of Hospitality, Bush Tav. Corn-st. Bristol, 2d and 4th W.
249 St. Peter's Lodge, King's Head, at Walworth, 3d M.
250 No. 1,
251 No. 2, } at Sweden
252 No. 3,

253 Golden Lion, at Neston, Cheshire, 1st F.
254 Lodge of Sincerity, Phœnix Inn, Fore-st. Plymouth Dock, 2d and 4th M.
255 Lodge of St. John, Fleece Tav. Manchester, last M.
1770.
256 L. of Perfect Harmony, at Mons, in the Austrian Netherlands
257 Lodge of Friendship, Bunch of Grapes, Limehouse-hole, 2d and 4th W.
258 Lodge of Prosperity, Globe Tav. St. Saviour's Ch. Yd. Southwark, 2d W.
259 St. Charles de la Concord, in the City of Brunswick
260 Lodge of Fortitude and Perseverance, Fox, Epsom, Th. nearest full M.
261 White Hart, Christ Church, Hants
262 Lodge of Concord, private Room, Barnard Castle, Durham, 1st Th.
1771.
263 Jerusalem Lodge, Crown-t. Clerkenwell-green, 1st and 3d W. Mast. L. 5th W.
264 Lodge of Industry, Ben Jonson's Head, Shoe-lane, 2d Th.
265 L. of Perfect Union, at Leghorn
266 Lodge of Sincere Brotherly Love, at ditto
267 Lodge of Perfect Union, St. Petersburgh
268 Lodge of Friendship, Prince George, Fore-st. Plymouth Dock, 1st and 3d W. l. F. Mast. L.
269 Junior Lodge, Kingston, No. 2, in Jamaica
270 Harmony Lodge, Kingston, No. 3, in ditto
271 St. James's Lodge, Montego-bay, No. 4, in ditto
272 Union Lodge, St. James's Parish, No. 5, in ditto
273 Lodge of Harmony, Bush, Carlisle, Cumberland, 2d W.
1772.
274 Rising Sun Lodge, at Fort Marlborough, in the East Indies
275 Lodge of Vigilance, Island of Grenada
276 Lodge of Discretion, ditto
277 Torbay Lodge, Crown and Anchor, at Paignton, in Devon
278 Union Lodge, at St. Eustatius, in the West Indies
279 Lodge of Candour, at Strasbourg
280 L. of Friendship, Shipwrights' Arms, Deptford-green, 2d Th.
281 Lodge at Speight's Town, in Barbadoes
282 Lodge of Concord, at Antigua
283 Lodge

(67)

283 Lodge of the Three Grand Principles, King's Head, Iſlington, Fr. on or near full Moon
284 *Royal Edmund Lodge, at Bury St. Edmunds, W. preceding or on full Moon*
285 Union Lodge, at Venice
286 Lodge at Verona
287 Lodge of Liberty, Half Moon, Weſt Smithfield, 1ſt Th.
288 Lodge of Unanimity, at Calcutta, 3d Lodge of Bengal
1773.
289 Lodge at Detroit, in Canada
290 *Apollo Lodge, at the Merchants' Hall, York*
291 *Lodge of Jehoſaphat, Rummer Tav. Briſtol, 1ſt and 3d W.*
292 Anchor and Hope, Calcutta, 6th Lodge of Bengal
293 Lodge of Humility with Fortitude, Calcutta, 5th Lodge of Bengal
295 *Lodge of Union, private Room, Hill Gate, Town of Gateſhead, Durham*
296 Williamſburg Lodge, at Williamſburg, Virginia
297 Botetourt Lodge, at Botetourt, Virginia
298 Lodge Frederick, at Caſſel, in Germany
299 L. of Good Friends, at Rouſſeau, at Dominica
1774.
300 *Lodge of Liberty and Sincerity, Crown Inn, Bridgewater, Somerſet, 2d and laſt Fr.*
301 *Lodge of Prudence, Boot & Shoe, Leigh, in Lancaſhire, W. next full Moon*
302 Unity Lodge, No. 2, at Savannah, in Georgia, 1ſt and 3d F.
303 Lodge of the Nine Muſes, No. 1, at Peterſburgh, in Ruſſia
304 Lodge of the Muſe Urania, No. 2, in ditto
305 Lodge of Bellona, No. 3, in ditto
306 Lodge of Mars, No. 4, at Yaſſy, in ditto
307 Lodge of the Muſe Clio, No. 5, at Moſcow, in ditto
308 *St. Bede's Lodge, Spread Eagle, Morpeth, Northumberland, 2d & 4th M.*
309 Lodge of Harmony, at Guernſey
1775.
310 *Durnovarian Lodge, Royal Oak, Dorcheſter, Dorſet*
312 *Sun and Sector, Workington, in Cumberland, 1ſt M.*
313 St. Jean de Nouvelle Eſpérance, in Turin
314 *True and Faithful Lodge, White Bear, W. of Malling, in Kent, laſt M.*

315 Grenadiers' Lodge, at Savannah, in Georgia, 1ſt and 3d C.
316 L. of True Friendſhip, with the 3d Brigade, 4th L. of Bengal
317 Green Iſland L. at Green Iſland, No. 8, in Jamaica
318 L. of Lucca; Pariſh of Hanover, No. 9, in ditto
319 Union L. at Savannah la Mar, No. 11, in ditto
320 Union L. at Detroit, in Canada
1776.
321 St. Andrew's L. Robin Hood, Charles ſt. St. James's, 4th M.
322 Royal York L. of Perſeverance, Coldſtream Reg. of Guards, 1ſt F.
323 *L. of Concord, at the Guildhall, Southampton, 1ſt F. Sum. 1ſt and 3d F. Win.*
324 *Royal Oak L. at the Royal Oak, Rippon, Yorkſhire, laſt S. Sum. 2d and laſt S. Win.*
325 L. of Honour, Bell, York ſt. Weſtminſter, 1ſt Tu.
326 *Induſtrious L. at the King's Head Inn, Canterbury, 1ſt and 3d Th.*
328 *King of Pruſſia, Penrith, in Cumberland, 2d W.*
329 *L. of United Friendſhip, Falcon Tav. Graveſend, 2d & 4th Th.*
1777.
330 L. of the Nine Muſes, Thatched Houſe Tav. St. James's ſtr. 2d F.
331 *Union L. Golden Lion, Thurſday Market, York, 1ſt & 3d M.*
332 *Social L. White Hart, Bocking, Eſſex, M. on or preceding full M.*
333 *Gnoll L. Ship and Caſtle, Neath, Glamorganſhire, 1ſt and 3d Tu.*
334 L. in the Iſland of Nevis
335 In the 6th, or Inniſkilling Reg. of Dragoons
1778.
337 L. at Meſſina, in Sicily
1779.
338 *Northumberland L. private Room, Alnwick, Northumberland, 2d M.*
339 L. of Independence, Vine Tav. Broad ſt. Ratcliff, 3d Tu.
340 Pilgrim L. Freemaſons' Tavern, Great Queen ſt. laſt W.
341 *L. of Fortitude, Bell Inn, Maidſtone, Kent, M. neareſt full M.*
1780.
342 L. of St. George, in the 1ſt Reg. of Dragoon Guards, 1ſt & 3d Th.
343 *St. Hild's L. private Room, S. Shields, Durham, 2d & 4th W.*
344 *Merchants' L. Star and Garter Tav. Liverpool, 1ſt & 3d Th.*
345 L. at Liebau, in Courland
346 L. at Naples

K

347 St.

164

347 St. Michael's L. private Room, Alnwick, Northumberland, 1ſt & 3d M.

348 St. George's Lodge, Town Hall, Doncaster, 2d W.

1781.

349 Alfred Lodge, Wetherby, Yorkſhire

351 Rodney L. Bull and Sun Inn, Kingſton upon Hull, 1ſt & 3d Tb. Win. 1ſt Tb. Sum.

352 Lodge Friendſhip, private Room, Dartmouth, Devonſhire, 1ſt, 3d, and laſt, Tb.

353 L. of Moral Reformation, Gun Tav. Deptford, 2d M.

354 La Loggia della Verita, Naples

355 Hiram's L. Ship Tav. Leadenhall ſtreet, laſt M.

1782.

356 St. George's E. York Militia L. in E. Riding Reg. of York Militia

357 Lodge of Science, Spread Eagle Inn, Saliſbury, 1ſt F. Win.

358 Old Britiſh and Ligurian L. Genoa

359 Mount Sinai L. St. John's, Antigua

360 L. of True Love & Unity, Brixham, Devon, 1ſt and 3d W.

361 L. of Peace, Joy, and Brotherly Love, Penryn, Cornwall

1783.

362 Mariners' L. New Dock, Liverpool, 1ſt and 3d Tb.

363 Minerva L. Hull, Yorkſhire

364 L. of Good Intention, in North, or 2d, Reg. of Devon Militia, 1ſt and 3d W.

365 Loyal L. Globe Inn, Barnſtaple, 1ſt and 3d Tb.

366 Apollo L. Parade Coffee Houſe, Saliſbury, 2d and 4th W.

1784.

367 L. at Placentia, Newfoundland

368 Holmeſdale L. of Freedom and Friendſhip, Bell, Ryegate, Surrey

369 Harmonic L. Buſh Inn, Dudley, Worceſterſhire, 2d & 4th Tb.

370 African L. Boſton, New England

371 Lodge of Truth, Cricketters, Richmond Green, 2d & 4th Tb.

372 Raby L. Raby Caſtle, Staindrop, Durham, 2d Tu.

1785.

373 Royal Gloucefter Lodge, Bell Inn, Gloucefter

374 L. of Concord, Old King's Arms, Plymouth Dock

375 La Parfaite Amitié, at Avignon, Languedoc

376 St. John's L. at Michlimacinac, Canada

377 Barry L. in the 34th Regiment

378 Rainsford L. in the 44th Regim.

379 Tyrian L. at the George Inn, Derby

381 Harbour Grace, Newfoundland

382 Trinity L. Golden Lion, Coventry, 1ſt & 3d Tb.

383 L. of Unanimity, private Room, Sadler ſt, Wells, Somerſetſhire, 1ſt & 3d Tb.

384 L. of Harmony, private Room, Hampton Court, occaſional

385 L. of St. George, White Hart, New Windſor, Berks

386 Thanet L. Parade Hotel, Margate, 2d and 4th W.

387 L. of Good Intent, Ship Tavern, Leadenhall ſt. 2d W.

388 White Lion, Whitchurch, Shropſh. Tb. previous to the full Moon

389 L. of Perfect Friendſhip, King's Head, King's ſt. Ipswich, 3d W.

390 Lodge of Unions, Spread Eagle, Pratt ſt. Lambeth, 1ſt M.

1786.

391 L. of Independence, Caſtle and Falcon, Watergate ſt. Cheſter

392 L. of Benevolence, Antelope Inn, Sherborn, Dorſet, 1ſt & 3d Tb.

394 L. of Friendſhip and Sincerity, Red Lion Inn, Shaftesb. Dorſet, 1ſt and 3d Tb.

395 Phoenix L. private Room, Portſm. occaſional

396 L. of the Black Bear, in the City of Hanover, (have met ſince 1774)

397 St. John's L. Golden Croſs, Broomſgrove, Worceſterſh. 2d & 4th M.

398 Carnatic Military L. at Vellore, No. 1, Coaſt of Coromandel

400 Hiram's L. at Gibraltar

401 L. of Goodwill, private Room, Braintree, Essex

402 L. of Sincerity, at the Buck and Vine, Wigan, Lancaſhire

403 L. of Harmony, at the Ship, Ormſkirk, Lancaſhire

404 Snowden L. at the Sportſman, Carnarvon, N. Wales

1787.

405 L. of St. Charles, at Hildburghauſen

406 St. Matthew's L. Barton upon Humber

407 Amphibious Lodge, at the Marine Barracks, Stonehouſe, near Plymouth

408 Newtonian L. Elephant & Caſtle, Knareſborough, 4th M.

410 L. of Trade & Navigation, New Eagle & Child, Northwich, Cheſhire, 1ſt W.

411 L. of Unity, Three Crowns Inn, Litchfield, 1ſt & 3d M.

412 Prince of Wales's Lodge, Star and Garter, Pall Mall

413 L. Aſtrea, at Riga, with permiſſion to aſſemble in the Dutchy of Courland

414 Royal

(69)

414 *Royal Denbigh L. at the Crown Inn, at Denbigh, N. Wales*

415 L. Abfolom, have met fince 1740, at Hambourg

416 L. St. George, ditto 1743, at ditto

417 L. Emanuel, ditto 1774, at ditto

418 L. Ferdinand Caroline, ditto 1776, at ditto

419 L. of Perfect Harmony, St. Thomas Mount, No. 3, Coaſt of Coromandel

420 L. of Social Friendſhip, at Madras, No. 4, ditto

421 L. at Trichinopoly, No. 5, ditto

422 L. of Social Friendſhip, St. Thomas Mount, No. 6, ditto

423 *Prince of Wales's L. White Hart, Gainſborough, Lincolaſhire, 3d M.*

424 St. Paul's L. Montreal, Canada

425 In the Regiment of Anhalt Zerbſt

426 L. of Unity, at Fort William Henry, in Canada

427 St. James's L. at Cataraqui, in ditto

428 Select L. at Montreal, in ditto

429 New Ofwegatchie L. in ditto

430 St. John's L. at Niagara, in ditto

1788.

432 *Wiltſhire L. at the Black Swan, Devizes, Wiltſhire*

433 L. of Unanimity, George Inn, Ilminſter, Somerfetſhire, Tu. before full Moon

434 *Salopian L. at the Fox, in Shrewſbury, 1ſt Tu.*

435 Bank of England L. Guildhall Coffee Houſe, King ſt. Cheapſide, 4th Th.

436 L. of Honour and Perſeverance, Ship, Cockermouth, Cumberland, 1ſt Th.

437 *Philanthropic L. Cock & Bell Inn, Milford, Suffolk, Tu. preceding or on full Moon*

438 *Duke of York's L. White Bear Inn, Doncaſter, 1ſt M.*

439 *Royal Yorkſhire L. Devonſhire Arms, Kighley, Yorkſhire, 1ſt M.*

440 The Old Globe L. Old Globe Inn, Scarborough

441 *Lodge of Napthali, New Market Inn, Mancheſter*

442 L. of Unity, Royal Oak, Mancheſter

443 L. of Union, St. John's Tavern, Mancheſter

444 L. of Fidelity, Thorn Inn, Burnley, Lancaſhire

1789.

445 *Egerton L. Red Lion Inn, Whitchurch, Shropſhire*

446 Star and Garter, Pall Mall

447 L. of Unity, at Dantzick

448 St. John's Lodge of Secrecy and Harmony, at Malta

449 County Stewards' L. Freemaſons' Tavern, Great Queen ſt.

450 At Fredericton, New Brunſwick, N. America

451 *Cambrian L. at the Swan Inn, Brecon, S. Wales, 3d M.*

452 *Royal Clarence L. White Horſe, Brightbelmſtone, Suſſex, 2d and 4th M.*

453 L. of Harmony, at the White Hart, in the Drapery, Northampton,

454 *Beneficent L. as the Angel, Macclesfield, Cheſhire*

455 *Royal York Lodge, Buſh Tavern, Corn ſt. Briſtol, 1ſt and 3d W.*

456 L. Frederick Charles Joſeph, of the Golden Wheel, at Mentz

457 *Wrekin L. at the Pheasant, Wellington, Shropſhire, M. previous to full Moon*

458 *L. of Tranquillity, Old Boar's Head, Mancheſter*

459 Independent L. at the Black Lion and Swan, Congleton, Cheſhire

460 Albion L. at Skipton, Yorkſhire

461 L. of Harmony, Bacchus, Halifax, Yorkſhire, 2d M.

462 L. Good Fellowſhip, Saracen's Head, Chelmsford, Eſſex, F. on or preceding full Moon

463 L. of Friendſhip, at the Angel, Oldham, Lancaſhire

464 L. of the North Star, at Fredericknagore, 7th L. of Bengal

465 Calpean L. at Gibraltar

1790.

466 Friendly L. King's Head Tavern, Holborn, 2d Th.

468 Harmony L. Dolphin Hotel, Chicheſter, Suſſex

469 *Royal Clarence L. George Inn, Frome, Somerſet*

470 Corinthian L. at the Ram Inn, Newark, Nottinghamſhire, M. near full Moon

471 St. John's L. at the Lion and Delphin, Market-place, Leiceſter, 1ſt W.

472 L. Archimedes, of the Three Tracing Boards, Altenburg, Germany

473 L. of the Three Arrows, at Nurnberg, ditto

474 L. of Conſtancy, at Aix la Chapelle, ditto

475 L. of the Riſing Sun, at Kempton, in Swabia, ditto

476 L. of the Temple of True Concord, at Caſſel, ditto

477 L. Charles of Unity, at Carlſruhe, ditto

K 2   478 L.

{ 70 }

478 L. of Perfect Equality, at Crey-feld, ditto
479 L. Aftrea, of the Three Elms, at Ulm, ditto
480 L. St. Charles of the Red Tower, at Ratibon, ditto
481 L. of Solid Friendship, at Trichinopoly, No. 7, Coast of Coromandc
482 Lodge of Benevolence, Red Lion, Stockport, Cheshire
483 Rein Deer Inn, Worcester, 2d and 4th Th.
484 Lodge of Fortitude, at the Golden Shovel, Lancaster

1791.
485 Silurean L. King's Head Inn, Kington, Herefordshire
486 L. of Friendship, Gibraltar
487 Bedford L. King's Arms, Tavistock, Devonshire, 1st and 3d W.
488 Lodge of Amity, Swan Inn, Rochdale, Lancashire
489 At Aberistwith, South Wales
490 L. of the Silent Temple, at Hildesheim, in Germany
491 Doric L. Ship Tavern, Grantham, Lincolnshire, 2d F.
492 St. John's L. at the Talbot, Henley in Arden, Warwickshire, 1st and 3d F.
493 Loyal and Prudent L. Leeds, Yorkshire
494 Lodge of Love and Harmony, Barbadoes.

1792.
495 At Bulam, on the Coast of Africa
496 North Nottinghamshire L. Town Hall, East Retford, 2d F.
497 Lodge of St. George, at a private Room, North Shields, Northumberland
498 Rawdon L. between the Lakes in Upper Canada
499 Faithful L. at Biddeford, Devon
500 L. of Prudence, at the Three Tuns, Halesworth, Suffolk
501 Man and Moon, St. Mary's, Norwich
502 L. of Love and Honour, Bell Inn, Shipton Mallet, Somerset, 2d and 4th Tu. Win. 2d Tu. Sum.
503 Royal Gloucester L. East street, Southampton
504 Samaritan L. at the Devonshire Arms, Kighly, Yorkshire
505 Philanthropic L. Devonshire Arms, Skipton, Yorkshire
506 L. of the Three Graces, Barnoldswich, in Craven, Yorkshire, 2d Sa.
507 Bermuda L. at St. George's, in Bermuda
508 Noah's Ark L. Canal Coffee House, Middlewich, Cheshire

509 L. of Unanimity, Stockport, Cheshire, 1st W. after full Moon
510 Urania L. Angel Inn, Glamford Briggs, Lincolnshire
511 L. of Harmony, Black Dog, Newchurch, Rossendale, Lancashire
512 Lodge of Fidelity, White Horse, Bear-lane, Leeds

1793.
513 White Hart, Huddersfield, Yorkshire
514 Union Lodge, Rose, Edgbaston st. Birmingham. W. on or before full Moon
515 Cambridge New Lodge, Red Lion, Cambridge
516 Shakespeare L. White Lion, Stratford upon Avon, Warwickshire
517 Rural Philanthropic L. Highbridge Inn, Huntspill, Somersetshire, Tu. preceding full Moon
518 At the Castle, Lord st. Liverpool
519 Scarsdale L. Angel Inn, Chesterfield, Derbyshire
520 The King's Friends Lodge, Three Pigeons, Nantwich, Cheshire
521 Union L. at Cornwall, in Upper Canada
522 St. John's L. of Friendship, at Montreal
523 Friendly Brothers L. at the Buck, Newcastle, Staffordshire, 1st W.
524 L. of Urbanity, Bear Inn, Wincanton, Somersetshire, 1st F.
525 Constitutional L. at the Tiger, Beverley, Yorkshire
526 Union L. Macclesfield, Cheshire, 1st Th.
527 Royal Brunswic Lodge, Royal Oak, Sheffield, Yorkshire
528 At Chunar in the East Indies, 8th Lodge of Bengal
529 L. of Mars, Cawnpore, 9th Lodge of Bengal
530 Witham L. Rein Deer Inn, City of Lincoln
531 L. of Unity, Half Moon, Marketplace, Yarmouth, Norfolk, M. nearest full Moon
532 L. of Harmony, Blue Ball, Rochdale, Lancashire
533 Royal Edward Lodge, Red Lion, Leominster, Herefordshire, 2d M.
534 L. of St. John, at the Grapes, Lancaster

1794.
535 Lodge of Emulation, Marquis of Granby, Dartford, Kent, Tu. nearest full Moon
536 L. of Minerva, King's Arms, Ashton under Line, Lancashire

537 The

(71)

537 *The Apollo Lodge, Angel, Alceſter, Warwickſhire, 1ſt and 3d W.*
538 *L. of Unity and Friendſhip, New Bear Inn, Bradford, Wilts*
539 *L. of Hope, at the Duke of York, Bradford, Yorkſhire*
540 *Benevolent L. at the Newfoundland Fiſhery, Teignmouth, Devon*
541 *L. in Cheſhire Militia*
542 *Philanthropic Lodge, Crown Inn, Kirkgate, Leeds*
543 *Crown Inn, Nantwich, Cheſhire, Th. near full Moon*
544 *Apollo L. White Lion, Beccles, Suffolk*

1795.

545 *L. of St. Winifred, King's Head, Holywell, Flintſhire*
546 *Alfred L. private Room, Leeds*
547 *St. Bartholomew's L. White Lion, Fazley, Tamworth, Staffordſhire, 2d Tu.*

548 *L. of Peace & Good Neighbourhood, Wynnſtay, Denbighſhire*

1796.

549 *Loyal Halifax L. Ring of Bells, Halifax, Yorkſhire, 3d M.*
550 *L. of Prince George, White Lion, Maworth, Yorkſhire, 1ſt W.*
551 *L. of Harmony, Fountain Tavern, Goſport*
552 *Perfect L. Horſe and Star, Woolwich*
553 *L. of Strict Benevolence, Maid's Head, Lynn, Norfolk*
554 *Veſtis L. of Peace and Concord, Wheat Sheaf, Newport, Iſle of Wight, 2d M.*
555 *Union L. Grapes Inn, Carliſle*
556 *Ebenezer L. Pately Bridge, Yorkſhire*
557 *South Saxon L. Star Inn, Lewes, Suſſex*

Tables of the Town, Country, and Foreign, Lodges, with Reference to the Numerical Liſt, by the Number of each Lodge.

Town-Lodges, according to their Days of Meeting.

MONDAYS.

1ſt.—5, 21, 180, 203, 238.
1ſt. & 3d.—18.
2d.—26, 322, 327, 380.
3d. & 4th.—2, 228.

3d.—7, 12, 110, 188, 249, 390.
4th.—20, 30, 50, 186, 142, 321.
Laſt.—355.

TUESDAYS.

1ſt.—135, 283, 325.
1ſt. & 3d.—4, 90, 142.
2d.—43, 95, 104, 178, 182, 231.

2d. and 4th.—32.
3d.—92, 183, 211, 339.

WEDNESDAYS.

1ſt.—134, 205, 236.
1ſt. & 3d.—1, 6, 57, 263.
2d.—29, 54, 68, 56, 258, 387.
2d. & 4th.—3, 257.

3d.—8, 113, 218.
4th.—55, 66, 117, 118.
Laſt.—340.

THURSDAYS.

1ſt.—14, 21, 25, 41, 49, 72, 97, 217, 287.
2d.—67, 215, 239, 264, 466.

2d. & 4th.—9, 23, 53.
3d.—128, 131, 169, 184.
4th.—60, 69, 435.

FRIDAYS.

1ſt.—171.———2d.—330.———3d.—27.———4th.—124.

TOWN

(72)

TOWN LODGES.

Bishopfgate ftr. 113
Bloomfbury High ftr. 328
Carnaby fq. 4
Cavendifh fq. 7
Cateston ftr. 12
Chancery lane, 20
Cheapfide, King ftr. 180, 435
Covent Garden, 131
Clerkenwell, 263
Charing Crofs, 134
Doctor's Comm. 18, 30
Eaft Smithfield, 29, 41
Fleet ftr. Silver ft. 15
—— Shoe lane, 264
Fifh ftr. Hill, 60
Great Queen ftr. 1, 2, 21, 23, 96, 205, 340, 449
Grofvenor fq. Brook ftr. 8, 68, 124
—— Mount ftr. 60
Goodmans F. Manfel ftr. 25
Haymarket, 71
Holborn, 14, 184, 217, 466

Iflington, 283
Lambeth Marfh, 50
—— Pratt ftr. 390
Leadanhall ftr. 53, 355, 387
Ludgate Hill, 242, 259
Limehoufe, 257
Oxford ft. Old Cavendifh ftr. 95
—— N. Audley ft. 97
—— Wells ftr. 288
Old ftr. Road, 118
—— Square, 183
Piccadilly, Dover ftr. 22.
—— Marybone ftr. 32
—— Halfmoon ftr. 69
—— Air ftr. 110
—— Burlington ftr. 128
Pall Mall, 27, 412, 446
Paddington, 55
Portland Road, 285
Rathbone Place, 182
Ratcliff, Broad ftr. 339
St. James's ftr. 1, 26, 54, 117, 171, 238, 330

St. James's ftr. Charles ftr. 321
Spitalfields, 169
Strand, Surry ftr. 43
Southwark, Joiner ftr. 66
—— Horfelydown la. 67
—— Tooley ftr. 178
—— Shad Thames, 203
—— Chriftchurch, 211
—— Bermondfey, 218, 231
—— St. Saviour's C. Y. 258
Soho, Old Compton ftr. 215
Smithfield, 287
Temple Bar, 236
Weftminfter, Palace Yd. 5
—— Downing ftr. 92
—— Crown ftr. 104
—— Whitehall, 180
—— York ftr. 325
Wapping, 9, 57
Whitechapel, Red Lion ft. 242
Walworth, 249

COUNTRY LODGES.

BERKSHIRE.

New Windfor		385

CAMBRIDGESHIRE.

Cambridge 106 515	Ifle of Ely	179

CHESHIRE.

Chefter 58, 123	Congleton	459
207, 391	Stockport 482	509
Nefton 253	Middlewich	508
Northwich 410	Nantwich 520	543
Macclesfield 454	Chef. Militia	561
526		

CORNWALL.

Falmouth 87	Scilly	235
Redruth 103	Penryn	361

CUMBERLAND.

Carlifle 273, 555	Penrith	328
Workington 312	Cockermouth	436

DERBYSHIRE.

Derby 379	Chefterfield	519

DEVONSHIRE.

Exeter 35, 146	Paignton	277
Plymouth 79, 137,	Dartmouth	352
140	Brixham	360
Stonehoufe 407	Devon. Militia	364
Plymouth D. 254,	Barnftaple	365
268, 374	Taviftock	487
New Ab. 141, 243	Biddeford	499
Topfham 177	Teignmouth	540
Tiverton 226		

DORSETSHIRE.

Pool 187	Sherborn	392
Dorchefter 310	Shaftefbury	394

DURHAM.

Stockton 19	BarnardCaftle	261
Swalwell 44	Gatefhead	295
Sunderld 121, 129	S. Shields	343
Darlington 144	Staindrop	372
Old Llvit 166		

ESSEX

FOREIGN

(74)

FOREIGN LODGES.

New Orleans Scottish Rite College
http://www.no-sr-college.com

Clear, Easy to Watch
Scottish Rite and Craft Lodge
Podcast & Video Education